Footfalls from the Land of Happiness
A Journey into the Dances of Bhutan

FOOTFALLS FROM THE LAND OF HAPPINESS

A Journey into the Dances of Bhutan

Karen Greenspan

ISBN: 978-0-578-45484-9

Cover and interior design by Gopa & Ted2, Inc.

Publisher's Cataloging-in-Publication Data

Names: Greenspan, Karen Elise., author.
Title: Footfalls from the land of happiness: a journey into the dances of Bhutan / Karen Greenspan.
Description: Includes bibliographical references and index. | New York, NY: Footfalls LLC, 2019.
Identifiers: LCCN 2019902507 | ISBN 978-0-578-45484-9
Subjects: LCSHArt and dance--Bhutan. | Dance--Bhutan. | Dance—Cross-cultural studies. |
Folk dancing—Bhutan. | Dance—Religious aspects--Buddhism. | Bhutan--Religious life and
ustoms. | BISACPERFORMING ARTS / Dance / Regional & Ethnic
Classification: LCCGV1703.B47 .G74 2019 | DDC793.3—dc23

First Edition

Printed in Malaysia

Contents

Acknowledgments

ONE OF MY favorite mental exercises is a Buddhist meditation in which one contemplates all the causes and conditions that have come together to bring one to the present moment and place. The reflection always makes me feel vastly connected and supported. So, here, I offer this contemplation in print with a heart full of gratitude and joy. I apologize in advance that I may have inadvertently missed many who deserve recognition.

I can't begin to thank Michael Harkavy enough for the selfless hours of thought, energy, and skill he gave to this book. He generously coached me with his intellect, expertise, and above all, his fervent belief in the book's merit and eventual fruition. Thank you!

I am deeply grateful to Khenpo Phuntshok Tashi, who patiently discussed the sacred dances with me, advising me on the dance masters I should meet and the sacred dances I should witness. He has read my manuscripts, guided me with suggestions over the years, and graciously contributed the foreword to this book. I offer my sincere gratitude to the Chakar Lama and his family for opening their home, temple, and traditions to me with great warmth and kindness. Thank you to Jamyang Choda, general manager of Yangphel Adventure Travel, who has gone far beyond the duties of travel arrangement and scouted out dance practitioners for me to interview, communicated and translated follow-up emails with them on my behalf, and supplied facts and data that were essential to the book. I offer immense gratitude to Younten Jamtsho, my first guide in Bhutan, who shared his sincere love of country and authentic spirituality, providing my initial entry into Buddhism and Bhutan. Thank you to Ugyen Yosar who provided helpful suggestions in addition to his expert guiding. And much gratitude goes to Singye Wangchuk for so much help in facilitating countless encounters and in translating interviews. I thank Tshering, vice principal of the Royal Academy of Performing Arts in Bhutan, who has helped me greatly in understanding the background of the Bhutanese folk forms and included me in many of RAPA's projects. Thank you to Geographic Expeditions and to Karma Lotey, CEO of Yangphel Adventure Travel, for expertly realizing my many unusual travel requests. *Kadinche la* (thank you) to the many dance and ritual practitioners of Bhutan who shared their personal stories, explanations, and dancing with me and who keep these treasured traditions alive.

Much gratitude goes to Joseph Houseal, creator of the invaluable Bhutan Dance Project through his organization Core of Culture. This research tool for accessing the dances and festivals of Bhutan has been invaluable to me. I truly appreciate how, over the years, Houseal has shared his knowledge and understanding of Bhutanese dance and Vajrayana Buddhism in terms that I could grasp. He has opened many doors for me with his unbridled love of dance, sincere advice, and enthusiastic encouragement. Dr. Judith Lynne Hanna's seminal work in dance anthropology provided my early inspiration for observing and investigating dance within the context of culture. I so appreciate her encouragement and validation as I pursued this work many years later. I am grateful to Tom Campbell, who is a most generous and constant Buddhist teacher and guide. Heartfelt thanks to the community of learners, spiritual friends, and educators at The Rubin Museum of Art and Tibet House. Both institutions are bounteous resources for my study of Buddhism and meditation. I am so thankful to Tanisha Jones, assistant curator at the Jerome Robbins Dance Division of the New York Public Library for her exceptional help. Much of my dance research is made possible by the knowledgeable and supportive curators and librarians at the NYPL Dance Division, the largest archive of dance material from all over the world. This institution is a temple of treasures for me.

I offer deep appreciation to Charles Harris at *Natural History Magazine*, Marvin Hoshino at *Ballet Review*, and Rabi Dahal and Sonam Pelden at

Tashi Delek, along with their talented colleagues, for their encouragement and uplifting presentation of my work in their excellent publications.

I owe a special thank you to Naomi Mindlin for her careful review of the manuscript and sharp copyediting skills and to Dr. Mona Schrempf for her generously contributed and important suggestions. I extend my appreciation to Mindy Aloff for her ideas, support and enthusiasm for the book. To Gopa Campbell, I offer immense respect and gratitude for transforming my written pages into an elegant design beyond my dreams.

I am indebted to my cherished friend and mentor Marilyn Katz, who constantly challenged me to write, read numerous drafts, offered her knowledgeable advice, and enthusiastically celebrated my successes along with her own. I offer my heartfelt thanks to Nancy Spriggs, who connected me with my first editor at *Natural History*. This sparked the magazine's publication of my first article on dance in Bhutan—one of my earliest footsteps toward the writing of *Footfalls from the Land of Happiness*. I give a bow to Nancy's daughter Barbara Gates, who has doled out her encouragement and inspired me with her own talented and sensitive writing.

I could never have pursued this labor of love without the unwavering support, love, humor, and companionship of my dear husband, Steven Abramson, who took the first steps into the "Land of Happiness" with me. Steven was and is my first and chief editor and continues to be my principal partner in all endeavors.

And finally, I thank my maverick mother, Hannah Galerstein. She shared with me her embrace of diverse flavors—in food, clothing, art, music, and dance. Her initial invitation to me when I was a child to join her circle of international folk dancers ignited my insatiable passion for the dances of all peoples. Thank you, Mom, for your dancing heart.

 I dedicate this book to dancers everywhere, that they may know that their activity has the power to effect positive change in themselves and in the world.

Foreword

It is said that the body of the superior spiritual practitioner, through his devotion, wears a hole, or indentation, upon the cushion through prolonged sitting in meditation day in and day out. At the same time, the middle-level practitioner often wears a hole in her walking shoes due to her devotion and numerous pilgrimages to the sacred sites. Lastly, the third level of spiritual practitioner wears a hole in the ritual drum through its use with the ritual bell in performing so many rituals for the benefit of all sentient beings.

THE BODY BECOMES sacred when it is utilized and set into movement performing the sacred expression called *cham*. These sacred dances are performed within the courtyard of the monastery, which serves as a real-life mandala (abode of the deities). In this way, the dancers' footsteps trace the footsteps of the enlightened beings and provide an opportunity for enlightenment not only for the dancers but also for those observing the ritual dance as well.

Bhutan is a small kingdom located in the Eastern Himalayas. It has become known for its aspiration for the happiness and well-being of its people through its policy of Gross National Happiness. Bhutan is also known as the sacred jewel of the Himalayas and the pure land of Guru Padmasambhava. Of course, these days modern Bhutan is connected to the wider world through the Internet, television, smart phones, and so on—yet as an antidote to these sophisticated modern technologies, which provide an onslaught of unrestricted information, the Bhutanese protect and immerse themselves in their precious cultural heritage through a calendar of sacred festivals, rituals, holy days, and national events during which cham and folk dances are performed. Given our Buddhist perspective, students are taught to use modern technology in a moderate way in order to enhance their lifestyle and for the purpose of education and communication without grasping and attachment to the tools.

According to Vajrayana Buddhism, the dancers' movements within the sacred cham are the gestures of the Buddha, and the sound of footfalls represents the speech of the Buddha. Performing this enlightened activity, the mind of the dancer takes on the mind of the Buddha. This means that through cham, the ordinary body, sound, and thought are transformed into the body, speech, and mind of the enlightened masters. Cham dancers are trained to dance fully, with mindfulness, within the mandala of primordial wisdom, and for the benefit of all beings. In doing so, they leave no trace of ego-centered emotion or attachment to worldly name and fame.

Karen Greenspan, a dance writer from New York City, visited Bhutan several times—not only to discover the treasure of sacred cham, but also to experience these dances on many levels. Based on her experiential understanding of this sacred part of Bhutan's intangible culture, she has generously shared her knowledge with others through this personal and heartfelt discourse on the dances of Bhutan. Karen has spent time learning the folk dances with Bhutanese artists, and interviewing dance masters—in particular the 90-year-old Chakar Lam Dorje, who, for many years, has been a cham dance master and the head lama of Chakar Lhakhang (Temple) in Bumthang.

In Vajrayana Buddhism, sacred dance is considered a skillful means to inspire or transport viewers to liberation, because by observing the cham, one witnesses the physical manifestation of the deities and their footsteps, which express the victorious celebration of wisdom and compassion over negative forces.

When reading through Karen's writings, I find myself transported into a state of deep mindfulness and reverie on the sacred dances of Bhutan and their deeper meaning. I trust that readers will also enjoy reading her work and discover much from her study and observations about this sacred art and practice that is so central to Bhutan's cultural heritage.

Khenpo Phuntshok Tashi

Director of the National Museum of Bhutan

Paro, Bhutan

May 8 2017

NOTE ON SPELLING

In the writing of Dzongkha, Tibetan, and Sanskrit words, I have tried to follow the popular Romanization used in English publications in Bhutan. As English is the language of educational instruction in Bhutan, there has been a drive to standardize the Romanized phonetic spelling of the national language. This spelling model, published in 1991, is not strictly adhered to. Many do not even know of its existence. Occasionally I refer to titles of works that were published before efforts at integrating standardization began. Some discrepancies are inevitable.

PART I:
Beginner's Mind

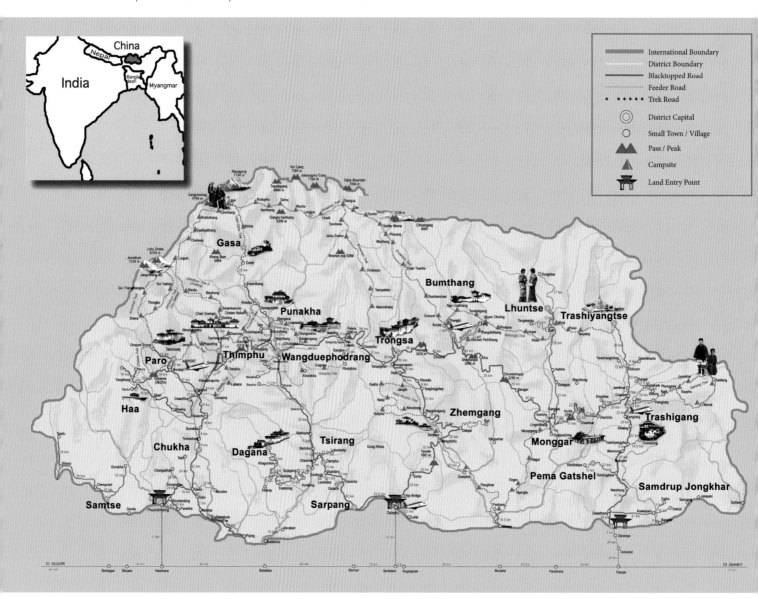

Introduction

A FOOTFALL, according to Webster's dictionary, is "the sound of footsteps." The chapters within this book are the echo, or ripple effect, of my footsteps of discovery through Bhutan. The reverberations were not just of my steps—but of the sacred dance steps that continually spin magic and meaning throughout the country of Bhutan, as well as into my life.

Being avid hikers, my husband and I signed up for a group hiking journey to Bhutan. We chose this destination as a means to experience the iconic Himalayas with the least amount of altitude sickness. Two weeks before departure, our travel company called to say that we comprised the entire group, but they would run the trip anyway. I must admit I was disappointed as I had always enjoyed the group aspect of hiking and adventure travel. After our arrival and first day with our Bhutanese guide, Jamtsho, I tumbled into bed thoroughly exhausted from the experience of all the undivided attention. But before long, I relished it.

Having never before traveled to Asia, the Himalayas, or a Buddhist country, I didn't begin to know what I didn't know—particularly when we attended our first *tshechu* (sacred festival) and witnessed the *cham* (sacred dances) of Bhutan. The printed itinerary listed it as a two-hour morning activity, but our guide could not pull us away. We were completely enthralled by the high ceremony, theater, and beautifully organic movement of these dances performed by Buddhist monks and laypeople. They are meant to liberate all from the human condition of suffering caused by the five poisons—hatred, attachment, ignorance, pride, and jealousy. The archetypal sounds and sights struck a primal chord that had long been dormant in me.

I had left the dance world 30 years before that trip after having danced and taught professionally. My dance roots were formed as a young child as I grasped the extended hands of the members of the international folk dance circle that my mother initially dragged me to every week at the local community center. I fell in love with the unusual and soulful melodies, the driving rhythms, and the thrill of moving in a connected group. Eventually, I pursued formal dance training at Southern Methodist University (SMU) and North Carolina School of the Arts and life in New York City as a modern dancer. Economic realities and nagging physical injuries demanded I move on, and so I did. But the blaring horns, vibrating cymbals, insistent drums, wrathful masks, and powerful physicality of the cham were going to pull me back to my original passion, my first language, *the* first language—dance. Here was a place where dance was an essential and sacred part of life—not just some discretionary diversion produced as a commercial venture only available to those who could afford the price of a ticket.

When I returned home from the trip, I devised a reason to return to Bhutan—to study their folk dances at the Royal Academy of Performing Arts (RAPA). I realized I would have to bridge the great gulf in my understanding of the culture. Then again, in Bhutan, to get anywhere in its geography of craggy mountains, high passes, verdant valleys, and rushing rivers, you have to build and cross bridges. In fact, one of the country's most revered folk and religious heroes is Thangtong Gyalpo, the Iron Bridge Lama. (This 14th-century religious teacher from Tibet was famous as an engineer who built many iron chain suspension bridges in the region and is also credited with originating *Achi Lhamo*—Tibetan folk opera.) So, I enrolled in courses and attended lectures on Himalayan Buddhism. When I discovered that the sacred dances were linked to meditative practices, I began attending weekly meditation sessions as well as developing my own personal practice.

My investigation of meditation led me to the understanding that the mindfulness meditation practices now quite common in the West were pioneered and preached by the Buddha some 2600 years ago as the most direct path to spiritual awakening. In the *Satipatthāna Sutta*, the Buddha's discourse on the practice of meditation, the first method of establishing awareness is through mindfulness of the body.[1] This important teaching communicates that the physical body provides a laboratory for discovery along the path toward enlightenment. In fact, mindfulness of the body is considered the simplest and most direct way to cultivate concentration and awareness. What is dance if not mindfulness of the body *in action*?

The prospect of commencing dance research reminded me of an assignment I had completed some 35 years earlier in a dance history class at SMU. We were asked to observe and write about a dance or ritual performance using a comprehensive dance observation tool. I remembered my enthusiasm for the project as I completed it in a dimly lit Greek restaurant in Dallas, Texas, bookishly jotting down notes on aspects of the belly dancer's performance! That observation tool influenced how I perceived dance, rituals, and even sporting events from that time onward. Of course, I had to locate this rubric these many years later. Thank heavens for Google! After patiently digging, I discovered that dance anthropologist Dr. Judith Lynne Hanna, research professor at the Department of Anthropology at the University of Maryland, was the author of this research tool that had made such an impression on me. I emailed her at the University of Maryland and she sent me a copy of those very guidelines, some suggestions, and her warm encouragement.

I reacquainted myself with the Jerome Robbins Dance Collection at the New York Public Library, which houses the largest, most comprehensive archive of dance material in the world. When I first arrived in New York as a dancer, I had spent wonderful hours there immersed in viewing recordings of the works of my favorite choreographers. Now I would do this again, as it is a mecca for dance research.

It was there that a helpful librarian directed me to a 24-inch Mac computer with colorful, attention-grabbing signage that said "Discover the Gods Who Dance" and offered, "You might be interested in taking a look at this." He set me up at the computer station, dedicated for use of the Bhutan Dance Database, with a pair of headphones and I was immediately enveloped by the primal sounds of the sacred Buddhist instruments. Colorful footage danced across the monitor, all of it transporting me to the stone courtyards beside the Bhutanese monasteries and fortresses halfway around the world. As I watched faces, dances, costumes, and scenery that I had seen for myself during my travels (as well as those that I had yet to see), I was drawn in for hours.

I wondered who made this window into that other universe possible and noticed a catchy logo on the sign above the computer for Core of Culture, the organization that had produced this phenomenal project. The founder and director of this organization, dedicated to the research and preservation of ancient dance forms, is Joseph Houseal—a whirlwind of intellect and creative energy. The Bhutan Dance Database contains more than 300 hours from five years of video recordings of the sacred and folk dances performed at the tshechus of Bhutan. It was part of the larger Bhutan Dance Project, which included a touring exhibition of Buddhist art and sacred dance presented by the Honolulu Academy of Arts. In 2005 the filming began in Bhutan and four years later copies of the Bhutan Dance Database were given to the National Library of Bhutan and the NYPL Dance Division. In 2010 the Dance Division purchased a Mac computer, to enable public access to the database, which is where I first encountered it. In the fall of 2013, the NYPL Dance Division made the database media files and catalogued information freely accessible to the public on the Internet—truly fulfilling its role as steward of the world's dance heritage.

When I returned from my second trip to Bhutan, I decided to write an article (my first) explaining the ideas behind the dances of Bhutan and my experiences learning some of them. I frequently referred to the Bhutan Dance Database, emailed follow-up questions to the faculty at RAPA, and began an email dialogue with Joseph Houseal to help me unpack the material I was observing and digesting. I had countless questions. The answers always pointed to the fact that dance in Bhutan is not a discretionary diversion as we in the West treat it. For them, it is an essential part of being Bhutanese and Buddhist—a spiritual practice that connects them to their history, land, and beliefs.

I have since used the Bhutan Dance Database for research pertaining to all of my projects on dance in Bhutan, preparing myself by learning the dances in advance of interviews and festivals. It has made all the difference to be able to walk into these situations with formulated questions and to be able to photograph the dances already knowing what I want to capture. One can access the Bhutan Dance Database online at https://digitalcollections.nypl.org/ and type "Bhutan Dance Project" into the search field.

One project led to another . . . and another. . . . Over time, it had utterly changed me. I became deeply involved in researching and writing about Bhutanese dance and that led to researching other cultures and their dances and, of course, writing about the wonder of it all. This small, barely known, Himalayan Buddhist nation that has put forth the concept of "Gross National Happiness" reawakened an essential aspect of myself. I found a kinship with this culture's innate understanding that the body and mind are indissolubly connected through dance. As I searched more deeply into Himalayan Buddhism to understand the sacred dances and their origins, I began to realize that here was a belief system that acknowledged and integrated body and mind into dance as a vehicle for transformation. This is something every dancer secretly understands, but it is all but forgotten in the West. The dances of Bhutan—inherited practices as well as living and evolving cultural expressions—are cherished as a key source of the society's happiness. Bhutan is a place where dance is not marginalized, but instead valued, elevated, and even sacralized—and has been for centuries. My engagement with this culture would eventually sensitize me to other ancient traditions that share this wisdom. To accommodate my insatiable curiosity and engage with dance and life in a different way, I would develop new skills of discovery—research, writing, dance photography, interviewing, Buddhism, meditation, and more. But that again has been part of the thrilling journey.

In the book, the dances serve as a window into the history and culture of Bhutan and the Himalayan Buddhist belief system that informs the overall experience of the country. The book is not intended to be a comprehensive catalog or encyclopedic account of the dances of Bhutan. It is, however, a selection of dances that is representative of some dance practices that are quite distinct to Bhutan as well as others that are central to Himalayan Buddhism. I unveil them along with their cultural context so you can appreciate these expressions in the fullest sense of this culture's way of "being" in the world.

Journeys rarely lead us to where we think we are going, and my outward journey to Bhutan, being no exception, spawned a vast and unbidden journey of transformation within. The footsteps were transitory events. The dances and their reverberations continue to vibrate through and transform my life.

CHAPTER ONE

The First Glimpse—Suspended amidst the Ancient, the Mystical, and the Modern

"*KUZUZAMPO LA*" or, "how is your honorary body after long sleep?" My earnest Bhutanese guide Jamtsho roughly translated this common greeting as he collected us from our hotel. The phrase is a warmly exchanged acknowledgment between friend and stranger alike. So I learned to let it roll off my tongue easily as I took my first steps into the faraway land and culture of Bhutan.

Shrouded in clouds and surrounded by mountain peaks, the tiny Buddhist nation of Bhutan is a developing country about the size of Switzerland and has a population of nearly 800,000. It is isolated by formidable geographic barriers—the Himalayas in the north and dense subtropical jungles in the south. For centuries the few roads and difficult geography protected it from colonization by foreign powers and, in more recent times, preserved its distinct culture and landscape from globalization and modern development. With two political giants for neighbors—China (which subsumed Tibet) to the north and India to the south—Bhutan walks a tightrope as it maintains its unique character and sovereignty. I landed on this destination simply as a means to experience the iconic Himalayas with the least amount of altitude sickness, never before having traveled to Asia and knowing nothing about Himalayan Buddhism.

We were staying in the town of Paro at a one-of-a-kind, Bhutanese-style property with architecture characteristic of traditional Bhutanese structures—notably, wooden interiors with densely carved designs and detailed, colorful iconographic painting. Traditional flute music permeated the ornately

FIGURE 2: The meditation hut of the female adept Yeshe Tsogyal clings to the rocks at Taktsang (Tiger's Nest).

decorated large public areas. Directly opposite our hotel room, the in-house Buddhist shrine room and attending monk were constant reminders of how different this place was from our usual Western surroundings.

The large picture windows of our enchanting room beckoned us outside to muse over a series of graceful, 30-foot-tall, white, prayer flags billowing in the wind on vertical poles. These are flags of mourning, whereas the horizontally strung, small, multicolored prayer flags fluttering at every bridge and mountain pass are so placed to spread prayers for happiness thanks to the action of the wind. At every turn, one stands in the presence of dark, rugged, rocky mountainsides, where faraway, isolated structures seem to cling to the most unlikely perches.

We headed out to visit Kyichu, one of the two first Buddhist temples in Bhutan. The modest structure is believed to have been built in the year 659 by the great Tibetan king and empire builder Songtsen Gampo, a committed convert to Buddhism. The Bhutanese credit him with introducing Buddhism to the region with his ambitious temple-building project to subdue a giant ogress who was thought to be impeding the establishment of Buddhism in Tibet. Jamtsho shared the oft-repeated story of Kyichu's origins that tells how the king built 108 temples in a single day to pin down the giant body of the demoness sprawling supine across the Himalayan region. Each temple, located throughout Tibet and Bhutan, was positioned to restrain a specific body part. Kyichu is reputed to hold down her left foot.

It is important to understand that although Bhutan and Tibet share a common Buddhist history and culture with attendant deities, saints, religious heroes and figures, and a geographic proximity; for the past 500 years, they have had separate and distinct political and sociocultural existences. In fact, there have been some extremely contentious episodes between the two countries. In spite of this, there has historically been a great deal of interchange between monks and lamas traveling back and forth seeking and bringing teachings from great masters located in one country or the other. To be clear, the Bhutanese maintain a strong identity as a separate people. This sense of a unique Bhutanese national identity and manner of conduct expressed through the structure of government, national celebrations, dress code, rituals, dances, and religious festivals was introduced and promoted by Bhutan's unifier and founding father, Zhabdrung Ngawang Namgyal, during his later years in the mid-1600s.

FIGURE 3: Kyichu Lakhang in Paro

Just a few generations after the launch of the Bhutanese national entity, the country fell into a long period of internal strife. In 1907, Ugyen Wangchuck, then governor of the district of Trongsa, united the country and was unanimously chosen to be the first *Druk Gyalpo* (Dragon King, which refers to the King of Bhutan, because Bhutan is called *Druk Yul*, or Land of the Thunder Dragon). The hereditary monarchy continues to the present even as Bhutan has transitioned to democracy, having become a constitutional monarchy in 2008.

Back at Kyichu, a family of mourners sat together on the flagstones of the temple courtyard and prepared a plate of food they would bring into the temple to offer their deceased relative at mealtime. They would sit in the temple with the uneaten plate of food for an appropriate length of time and then feed it to the ever-growing population of stray dogs. This ritual is performed three times a day for 49 days, to support the deceased through the in-between state, or *bardo*, the period following one's death until the moment of conception in one's next life. For the Bhutanese it is extremely important to usher one's relatives toward a "good rebirth."

After removing our shoes at the doorway, as is customary, we entered the dimly lit temple—heavy with the scent of incense, butter lamps, old fabric, and books. Villagers entered the intimate space making the requisite prostrations—three to the master lama and then three more to the Buddha. The lama sat cross-legged on a cushion opposite the central statues and altar. Directly in front of him was a small table of ritual implements (bell and dorje scepter) and a horizontal, loose-leaf tablet of ritual text. Poised to play the sacred instruments at precise moments during the liturgy, several monks sat to the side of the lama.

The monks had just finished their "tea break" and began blowing the five-foot-long horns and beating the drums with long hooked sticks as the master lama chanted Buddhist prayers in a deep, rhythmic drone. In the Himalayan Buddhist tradition, the drum represents wisdom and the hooked drumstick signifies compassion. Each drumbeat unites wisdom with compassion—to create self-arising awareness in the listener. Every time they started a new prayer the horn blowing would recommence with their resonating ancient sounds. Jamtsho informed us that this was one of the "auspicious" days of the month, so extra prayers and special offerings were added to the usual regimen. The Bhutanese make many decisions based on astrology and divination, and so the 8th, 10th, 15th, and 30th days of each month are deemed auspicious. According to their flexible calendar system, astrologers have the discretion of adding or deleting days and/or months to the calendar year for the sake of a successful outcome.

The many primeval sounds, smells, and sights flooded my senses upon entering the mysterious universe of a Himalayan Buddhist temple. The darkened interior of Kyichu houses the exotic golden statues of the serene Buddha; the beloved mustached saint, Guru Rinpoche; and an evocative Avalokiteshvara. This last statue, of the Deity of Infinite Compassion, was rendered with eleven heads, one thousand arms, and an eye engraved on each hand to enable him to accomplish the endless task of liberating all beings from suffering.

The story is told that Avalokiteshvara couldn't fully fathom the needs of the suffering multitudes, so his head cracked into eleven pieces to better hear and comprehend their cries. Then grasping the magnitude of his job, he was so overwhelmed that his mentor, Amitabha Buddha (Buddha of Comprehensive Love), invested him with one thousand arms and eyes to help him reach out to all who suffer.

The blinding daylight jolted us back into the outside world with its more mundane sights as we ambled along a farm road. Most paths are farm roads, since some 60 percent of the population is engaged in agriculture. Roosters crowed a serenade as we passed prematurely wrinkled and weathered old men and women hauling heavy loads of firewood on their backs. A younger couple languidly prodded their cow toward home while little children with cute, rosy faces and runny noses playfully interacted with us while laughing and running. "*Kuzuzampo la*"—I practiced the strange, lilting phrase, repeating the greeting to everyone we passed. They responded pleasantly without seeming the least bit impressed or surprised.

We continued our walk and I asked Jamtsho about his family. The monks had renewed their horn blowing and drumming, faintly audible in the distance. Jamtsho explained that his two sisters were both married to the same high lama who is a reincarnation of a previous high lama. This simple landscape and sincere discussion were only interrupted by an occasional cell phone call from my guide's travel office and his new bride.

CHAPTER TWO

Reincarnation for Dummies

T HE SEPARATION of Church and State, so basic to the fabric of life in the United States, is not the case in Bhutan. Bhutan is a Buddhist country, where the principles and philosophy of the religion form the bedrock and bulwark of the people's culture, daily lives, historical frame of reference, and worldview.

A basic tenet of Buddhism and the pan-Indian philosophies that preceded it is the belief in rebirth, or reincarnation. It is a product of the Indian understanding of time, which is perceived as circular and infinite—an eternity of cycles within cycles. Robert Thurman, eminent scholar of Tibetan Buddhism at Columbia University, explains in the background chapter to his translation of *The Tibetan Book of the Dead*, that rebirth is a Buddhist belief "that animate beings exist along a continuum of lives, and that the death, between, and rebirth processes follow a predictable pattern." He continues, saying that Buddhists act on this "perspective in a practical manner, using their lifetimes to educate themselves to understand the world and to prepare for death and future lives by improving their ethical actions, emotional habits, and critical insight."[2] Some of the Bhutanese sacred dances, described in the following chapters, deal with this very subject.

This nationally accepted and deeply ingrained life view came as a huge surprise to me, challenging my Western secular sense of things. I realized as I trekked across Bhutan's guru- and monk-trodden footpaths, listening to fantastic tales of folk heroes, history, current events, public policy, and everyday discourse, I would need to assume a different frame of reference in order to understand the conversation.

A teaching that resonated with me and gives a sense of the depth of this concept of rebirth is that every sentient being is your mother from a previous life. This idea informs how Buddhists believe one should treat all living things with kindness and compassionate love. There is no question as to how much respect, love, and care is owed the person who brought you into the world and then raised, supported, and nurtured you until you could sustain yourself. Given the rebirth construct, we have lived countless previous lives and had countless nurturing, loving mothers. Therefore, every living being today *could be* or *is* your mother from one of those previous lives. At first, I could not quite discern whether this was understood literally or conceptually. Either way, this thought framework gives a different magnitude to the importance of showing all creatures kindness and compassion. It is such a powerful concept that, for centuries, great Buddhist teachers have devised meditation techniques for cultivating love, kindness, and compassion based on visualizing all beings as one's own loving and selfless mother.

If every sentient being is your mother from a previous life, then killing animals, even for food, is clearly contrary to Buddhist principles. One day while hiking, we came across a dead bird on the trail. Jamtsho carefully picked it up and gently placed it on the branch of a shrub. He explained the teaching after he did this, saying this was a more dignified place for the bird. This sincere gesture of care and respect for what I considered a dead bird was an appropriate action and a living example of this belief system.

TRULKUS CAN BE COMPLICATED

Woven into the Himalayan Buddhist concept of reincarnation is the principle of recognized rebirth of a previous, exalted lama—also called a "reincarnate lama," or *trulku*. The process by which a trulku is identified is an established part of the culture that evolved in Tibet in the 13th century as a means to deal with the issues of succession in religious leadership and power. Typically, a lama may communicate to his closest protégé when and where he will take rebirth so that two or three years after a lama's death, a delegation of monks from his monastery will begin the search based on the forecast he gave. They identify prospective young children and submit them to tests and interviews that either prove or disprove their venerated identity.

True lamas are revered as incarnated enlightened beings, or *bodhisattvas* (already-enlightened beings who choose to continue to be reborn in order to aid all sentient beings on the path to enlightenment). Not many of us in the West occupy ourselves with aspirations of "enlightenment." So what does this concept (also referred to as "awakening," "realization," or "buddhahood") actually mean within the Buddhist context? Robert Thurman has described it as "expanded identification and at-oneness with all of existence; knowing what everyone and everything in the universe feels at all times; interconnection and interflowing with all beings."[3] In other words, enlightenment dissolves all barriers between self and other, giving rise to a state of active compassion for all beings, which are viscerally experienced as part of oneself.

The word "trulku" is Tibetan for the Sanskrit term "*nirmānakāya*" and refers to the physical, human manifestation of a *buddha*, or awakened being. In Himalayan Buddhism, the historical figure, Siddhartha Gautama Buddha, was not the only buddha. There were others in the past and will be others in the future. In fact, all human beings are considered to have buddha potential, for we have an essential "buddha nature" that simply needs to be cultivated. As such, it is completely understandable that trulkus should know and choose the optimal conditions under which to reincarnate to continue their unfinished work in the world.

Once a reincarnate lama is identified, a time is negotiated between the monastery leadership and the child's parents for the child to be taken to a monastery. There, he will be formally recognized as a trulku by a high lama in an elaborate ceremony and educated in accordance with his historical potential and position. This is how His Holiness the Dalai Lama was chosen and educated for his significant role. In this way, children are trained and molded for leadership from a very young age by the very people who are believed to have been the trulku's own students in his former life. It is a perfect circuit of knowledge transmission and preservation.

There have been instances of fraudulent claims as well as rival contenders for trulku status for a particular high lama. The story of Zhabdrung Ngawang

Namgyal, unifier and first ruler of the Bhutanese nation (see chapter 5) is such a case. To complicate things further, after his death, there were three claimants to his reborn identity. The compromise reached was for all three to be recognized as simultaneous rebirths generated separately—a body reincarnation, a speech reincarnation, and a mind reincarnation. This system of multiple reincarnations (body, speech, and mind) has proliferated in Bhutan.

Some of the intricacies of the trulku concept were underscored for me a year and a half later, after my second trip to Bhutan. The vice principal of the Royal Academy of Performing Arts (RAPA), Tshering, provided some background on a very simple folk dance I had learned, *Thrung Thrung Karmo*, about the valued and protected Black-Neck Cranes. Tshering (many Bhutanese have no last name) explained that the Pedtsheling Trulku of Bumthang composed the song. By virtue of the fact that the composer was a trulku, I knew he was a greatly respected holy man in the Bhutanese culture. I recalled that one of the RAPA faculty musicians had mentioned the name Pedtsheling Trulku with a tone of deep respect. So I wanted to know who he was. When did he live? What did he mean to the Bhutanese people? I had no context in which to place this lama/composer.

I emailed Jamtsho to see if he could enlighten me further on the subject. The next morning I was hopeful as I opened his emailed response. I laughed out loud. It was NOT an answer I expected! Jamtsho wrote, "Regarding the Pedtsheling Trulku, do you know which one—because he has a series of reincarnations and there are a few songs written by them."

CHAPTER THREE

Gross National Happiness—Outgrowth of Buddhism

A CUSTOMARY PRACTICE in Buddhist meditation is to wish for all beings to have happiness and the causes of happiness and to be free from suffering and the causes of suffering (two of the Four Immeasurables).[4] This Buddhist ideal of promoting happiness—personal and societal—as a mechanism for the liberation of all beings from suffering has led the modern nation of Bhutan to embrace a governmental-economic policy that they call—using the English term and acronym—Gross National Happiness (GNH). Bhutan's fourth king, Jigme Singye Wangchuck (b. 1955), initiated the idea shortly after his coronation in 1974. He later insisted that Bhutan become a constitutional monarchy in 2008, and then abdicated the throne in favor of his son Jigme Khesar Namgyel Wangchuck (b. 1980).

At first, GNH was simply a guiding principle asking, "Does this really promote the happiness of the people?" that the king and ministers considered with respect to decisions about policy and development. As the philosophy moved beyond Bhutan and was discussed in global fora, the outside scrutiny made it imperative that they flesh out happiness metrics with quantitative indicators. A strong internal debate ensued as to whether developing such indicators would lead them to succumb to a materialist view of what constitutes happiness. The country's leaders understood that many elements of value are not so easily quantifiable.

Today GNH provides explicit criteria to guide and measure the growth and development of the country. At its core are four priorities—equitable and sustainable development; protection of the environment; the preservation and promotion of Bhutan's unique cultural heritage (the tshechus, with their cham, are an example of the intangible cultural heritage that GNH seeks to nurture and protect); and provision of good, responsive governance. Through a national survey conducted and evaluated at regular intervals, the GNH Index measures nine domains of happiness and satisfaction of the Bhutanese people, including psychological well-being, community vitality, and cultural diversity and resilience. Similarly, all policies and projects are subjected to a strict GNH screening tool to assess their impact on GNH markers (for example: effects on population stress levels, opportunities for cultural participation, facilitation of physical exercise, impact on the environment) thereby determining their acceptance or rejection.

The fourth king and creator of the GNH concept more recently offered, "Today Gross National Happiness has come to mean so many things to so many people, but to me it signifies simply development with values. Thus for my nation today Gross National Happiness is the bridge between the fundamental values of kindness, equality, and humanity and the necessary pursuit of economic growth. GNH acts as our national conscience guiding us toward making wise decisions for a better future."[5]

Over the years, I have heard Westerners question whether GNH is a gimmicky salve for the people's lack of material comforts and development. We can't abide that another culture might be quite happy without subscribing to our measurements of success. However, the Bhutanese understanding of happiness is somewhat different from the Western interpretation, which is more based on the ability to meet materialist ideals and less on qualitative factors. The Bhutanese take a holistic attitude that is based on a socially interdependent sense of sufficiency and community. In other words, it is a happiness that is mutually created and shared. Recognizing this, the governmental GNH policy promotes opportunities for multigenerational integrity, community and family interaction, access to nature, and cultural immersion.

Finally, the United States is starting to have this discourse—led by universities now offering courses on happiness. They are responding to the pervasive "unhappiness epidemic" on campuses characterized by feelings of hopelessness, depression, stress, and an inability to function. Although Bhutan has been pondering happiness for several decades, concern has arisen that the country will lose its traditional and spiritual character as it adopts a greater consumer economy with the attendant appetite for material goods, along with feelings of discontent and dissatisfaction. Bhutan only recently opened itself to the outside world by joining the United Nations in 1971, building its first airport in 1983, and introducing television and the Internet in 1999. Time will tell how these interactions with the outside world and their snowballing developments will affect the reality of life for the people and the country.

For now, Bhutan is unique in that it has both a religious and political imperative to honor and protect both its natural environment and its dances.

PART II:
The Real Journey Begins

CHAPTER FOUR

Into the Mandala

WHEN WE EMERGED from the clouds and descended into the Paro Valley, it looked as though the wing of the plane would surely brush against the steep, rocky mountainside. Just then Bhutanese flute music piped in over the intercom, and our metal bird began her elegant and carefully calibrated dance with the mountains, gracefully gliding to the valley floor. I was back!

Bhutan had been tugging at me ever since I left its airspace the previous year. It originally attracted me because of the natural beauty of its ever-present guardians, the Himalayas. Then I discovered its resonant political discourse and singular dance culture. So I returned a year later with a twofold plan. I would attend the Paro *Tshechu*, or sacred dance festival honoring Guru Rinpoche, the saint who played a pivotal role in bringing Buddhism to Bhutan from India. In addition, for me, having a background of years performing and teaching international folk and modern dance, the highlight of the journey would be to study Bhutanese folk dance at the Royal Academy of Performing Arts (RAPA). Although I would have preferred to learn the sacred dances, they are performed exclusively by men and I knew the dance masters would never agree to teach them to me. I had also seen some of the folk dances performed the previous year at the Punakha Tshechu and wanted to experience the lyrical grace of the movements to the haunting melodies. Since both men and women perform the folk dances, I assumed my request to learn them would be acceptable—and it was. So I arranged to take lessons at RAPA.

The Tshechu

The next morning we joined the throngs of locals making their way to the outdoor grounds beside the Paro *Dzong* (fortress/monastery complex) for the Paro Tshechu. Scanning the scene, we could see young kids happily meeting up with their friends, old folks—their teeth stained red from chewing betel nut—spinning prayer wheels, young women carrying babies in woven wraps, men dressed in the traditional *gho* (a knee-length, colorfully woven belted robe) clutching their cell phones, and red-robed monks moving about with energy and purpose. The crowd was anticipating the tshechu processions, sacred dances, folk dances, and climactic unfurling of a giant cloth mural of Guru Rinpoche.

The tshechus of Bhutan are colorful spectacles that meld country fair, family picnic, historical reenactments, monks' ritual and ceremony—all in the spirit of collective renewal and blessings. "Tshechu," which means 10th day, is an established way the Bhutanese honor Guru Rinpoche, who, it is told, before departing earthly existence, promised to return on the 10th day of each lunar calendar month to dispel the suffering of the people. The fourth *Druk Desi* (secular ruler of the country), Gyalsey Tenzin Rabgye (1638–1696), institutionalized these sacred dance festivals to promote a sense of national identity and cohesion in the newly unified country and to patronize (through sacred danced ritual) the protector deities who safeguarded the country from external enemies and who were still needed to do so. These holy day traditions were adopted from *Nyingma* (oldest school of Himalayan Buddhism) observances and core repertoire already in existence in Tibet.

Just as today we might send our brightest young people abroad for training in some advantageous technology, Tenzin Rabgye dispatched some of the most talented monks under the leadership of Ugyen Tshering to Tibet to acquire further training in the transformative spiritual "technology" of that time and place—*cham* (sacred dance). These monks returned to Bhutan, performed these sacred dances in the main dzong in Thimphu (the current capital), and taught them to many other learned masters expanding the already-present cham repertoire in Bhutan. This caused the performance of cham to flourish and spread to other communities. In recognition of Ugyen Tshering's expertise, Tenzin Rabgye appointed him the nation's first *champon* (cham master).

Today the principal monasteries throughout the country host an annual tshechu, each at a different time of year, creating a yearly calendar chock-full of festivals. In a sense, Guru Rinpoche does return every month.

The main attraction at the tshechus is the cham, which can be distinguished in terms of their function: dances of offering and invocation; purificatory dances that cleanse the environment and renew the community through the subjugation and expulsion of negative forces; and narrative, didactic dances derived from Buddhist texts about principal saints and deities that teach compassion for all sentient beings. Originating as much as 1300 years ago, cham are performed by dancers who are frequently masked and wear decorated silk costumes. The dancers sometimes carry iconographic props or ritual imple-

FIGURE 4: An atsara keeps the crowd smiling at the Punakha Tshechu.

ments and may play drums, cymbals, or bells. They are accompanied by monk musicians chanting and playing the long horns, oboes, cymbals, drums, and conch shells.

One of the cham featured at the Paro Tshechu is a well-known, three-hour dance-drama called *Bardo Raksha Mangcham* (Dance of the Judgment of the Dead). Pages 28–33 contain a description of this cham.

A wonderful quality of the Bhutanese people is that they do not take themselves too seriously. In the midst of the sacred cham there are always the *atsaras* (jesters) in bright-red masks poking fun at dancers and audience members alike. In addition to carrying out their useful function of fixing loose or crooked costumes on the dancers, they romp around performing slapstick routines, hitting up tourists for donations, and bopping people playfully over the head with large wooden phalluses.

Bardo Raksha Mangcham (DANCE OF THE JUDGMENT OF THE DEAD)

THIS DRAMATIC WORK illustrates a journey through the *bardo*, a dream-like, in-between state that Buddhists believe all beings traverse after death and before their next rebirth. There they are judged by *Shinje* (Lord of Death) to determine whether they will be liberated to higher realms of existence upon their rebirth. Played out as a courtroom trial, the dance dramatizes the principle of *karma*—every action, both good and bad, produces relative consequences within the cycle of continuity.

The master of ceremonies for this courtroom drama is *Raksha Lango*, an ox-masked dancer who represents the minister of justice. The dance includes a scary-looking, black-masked prosecutor *Due Nagpo* (Black Demon); a white-masked defense attorney *Lha Karpo* (White God); a black-robed, sinful man *Nyalbum*; a white-robed, virtuous man *Palkyed*; a full jury of 23 animal-masked dancers with symbolic props (a set of scales, a lasso, a mirror of fate) representing the assembly of bardo deities; and an oversize costume-puppet of the Lord

FIGURE 5: (Opposite) Raksha Lango, the ox-masked dancer, is the master of ceremonies for this courtroom drama. (Punakha Tshechu)

FIGURE 6: (Above) Animal-masked jurors make their entrance. (Punakha Tshechu)

of Death with his attendants and angels. This didactic dance-drama addresses the universal preoccupation with the here-after. The Bhutanese believe that by viewing this cham, they will become aware of what to expect upon death and won't be frightened or distracted by the deities they will encounter as they proceed through the bardo and make choices that will influence their next rebirth.

While Nyalbum sits before the jury of animal-masked dancers, the festival attendees line up around the periphery of the dance ground and go before Lord Shinje and his attend-

ing monks to receive blessings, a prayer cord (to wear), and a sprinkle of holy water. Sometimes herbal pills made by the monastery monks are also dispensed providing another layer of benefits to the faithful—the promise of good health and longevity.

FIGURE 7: (Opposite) Lord Shinje is carried in by an entourage of monks and attendants.

FIGURE 8: (Above) Animal-masked dancers represent the assembly of bardo deities.

In one of the more comical moments, the villain tries to make a run for it and escapes into the audience. All the ministers of the court run after him until they haul him back onstage to stand trial. He pulls this trick three times! This varies from one performance to another. He is eventually convicted and dragged off on a long, black, cloth runner to a "lower realm."

The dance is considered a *tercham* (see following section) revealed by Terton Karma Lingpa (1326–1386) as a text called the *Bardo Thodroel*, which translates as "Liberation through Hearing during the Intermediate States" (known in the West as the *Tibetan Book of the Dead*). During the period of mourning rituals, this text is recited aloud to help guide

the consciousness of the deceased swiftly through the liminal states of bardo and ultimately to liberation from rebirth (or at least to rebirth in the human realm, which is viewed as the best opportunity for eventually attaining liberation). See the dance for yourself at https://digitalcollections.nypl.org/items/1eeacad0-e7f0-0130-d210-3c075448cc4b.

FIGURE 9: (Opposite) The courtroom trial is overseen by Raksha Lango. (Jampa Lhakhang Drub)

FIGURE 10: (Above) Festival attendees form a line and go before Lord Shinje to receive blessings during the dance-drama. (Jampa Lhakhang Drub)

Buddhism Arrives in the Himalayas

As mentioned earlier, Bhutanese mark the introduction of Buddhism into their country with the seventh-century Tibetan king, Songtsen Gampo, who promoted his new religion by building temples across the Himalayan region, two of which still exist today in Bhutan and are revered places of worship (see chapters 1 and 10). Buddhism gradually absorbed, transformed, and integrated the indigenous religious practices of the region under its own umbrella. A century later, the new religion solidified its hold when the tantric master and highly mythologzied figure Padmasambhava, better known in Bhutan as Guru Rinpoche, was invited to Tibet and Bhutan.[6] The Bhutanese believe he traveled throughout the area performing miraculous feats: flying on the back of a tigress, subduing opposing deities by performing cham, and converting enemies to eternal protectors of Buddhism.

FIGURE 11: Guru Rinpoche painted on a rock

Guru Rinpoche, whose life story exceeds the bounds of knowable history, is believed to have been active in the eighth century. Early texts found in the Dunhuang caves (in northwest China along the Silk Road network) recount his practice, mastery, and dissemination of a new school of Buddhism that was emerging in India between 500 and 1000 C.E. called Vajrayana or Tantra (the diamond or thunderbolt path, or vehicle). *Vajra* in the word "Vajrayana" was originally the thunderbolt-scepter of the Hindu god Indra. A symbol of impregnable strength, it evolved into the sacred implement of the same name, and is frequently used in rituals and cham as well as depicted in tantric Buddhist artwork. Vajrayana is based on belief in the possibility of accelerated progress toward enlightenment through personal transformation rather than the necessity of suffering through eons of endless rebirths. The Buddhist texts upon which the Vajrayana School is based are called *tantras*—hence the adjective, tantric. These texts are further developments of the earlier *sutras*, which record the discourses of Buddha Shakyamuni, in which he disseminated the fundamental teachings of his philosophy. Vajrayana requires the guidance of a teacher, or guru, as the practitioner identifies with a meditation deity (*yidam*) through elaborate visualizations, the recitation of *mantras* (sacred syllables) and the use of gestural and ritual supports. These Deity Yoga practices enable the meditator to transcend their own shortcomings and internalize the deity's divine qualities of wisdom, compassion, generosity, equanimity, and so on— part of the transformative work necessary to cultivate enlightenment.

Cham as Vajrayana Practice

Cham is an essential component of Vajrayana Buddhist ritual as well as an important public performance. As such, it pervades the Bhutanese cultural landscape. Some cham are derived from the tantric Deity Yoga practices (mentioned above) through which Buddhist practitioners transform themselves into an embodiment of the deities in order to overcome outer and inner obstacles to enlightenment. These have been passed down according to tradition, following Guru Rinpoche's example, for generations—from empowered lineage holders to their disciples. In fact, each monk dancer must be initiated into the particular dance of a deity by a senior monk before he may perform the dance—just as a practitioner must receive initiation into a particular Deity Yoga practice before undertaking that meditation practice. Before performing these ritual dances, the monks conduct religious ceremonies and meditation to personify the qualities in body and mind of the deity they will represent to the public. By wearing the costume and the consecrated mask, carrying the specific ritual implements in their hands, performing *mudras* (symbolic gestures that physically integrate the practitioner with the visualized action during Vajrayana ritual and worship[7]—different from the narrative or decorative hand gesture vocabularies used in Indian or Southeast Asian classical dance forms), reciting sacred mantras, and developing focused concentration, the dancers "embody" the deity and are supposed to remain undistracted by extraneous thoughts or external occurrences. Their costumes—long, full, silk-brocade robes—are similar to those of other northern Buddhist countries.

Other cham, called *tercham* (revealed treasure dances), are considered to have been rediscovered by treasure revealers (*terton*) in texts that Guru Rinpoche intentionally hid centuries earlier throughout the landscape of the Himalayas or in the minds of his disciples in anticipation of the people's spiritual needs in later times. Some tercham were revealed through visionary experiences during dreams or meditations and are called "mind treasures." The treasure revealers have long been revered for having discovered these concealed teachings, and some of their lineages exist until today. One of the most beloved and influential treasure revealers was Pema Lingpa (1450–1521), who is credited with transmitting cham masterpieces from his visions.[8] His treasure dances are now performed at every tshechu throughout Bhutan. Even the costumes he envisioned are used today in many of the other revealers' tercham. These short, colorful costumes, as well as the dances, are distinctly Bhutanese.

Another 15th-century treasure revealer, Kunga Gyeltshen, dreamt how the dance medium could be used to teach the deeper mysteries of Buddhism. In Bhutan, sacred dance has been for centuries the medium used for imparting religious and cultural knowledge to the general public, and it still is.[9] Before the second half of the 20th century, literacy was imparted in the monasteries and to a few elites. The general population was mostly illiterate and engaged in a subsistence agrarian lifestyle. Moral values and traditions were transmitted through storytelling, ritual observance, and cham. Bhutan's third king, Jigme Dorji Wangchuck (r. 1952–1972), introduced public education in the 1960s, setting in motion a different paradigm for acquiring knowledge and skills. Now, even with the benefits of modern education, the populace still enjoys an annual dose of multisensory religious and cultural messaging through attending the tshechus and viewing the dances.

Still other cham are dance-dramas that retell sacred biographies (*namthar*) or folk tales rooted in religious and cultural values. An example is *Shawa Shachi Cham* (The Dance of the Stag and Hounds), a famous dance-drama that shows how the master yogi Milarepa (c. 1052–c. 1135) converted a non-Buddhist hunter into a religious man. Although the tantric cham are performed by monks, lay people traditionally perform tercham and the dance-dramas. All cham are deemed equally sacred in terms of generating merit for the performer and viewer. The mere viewing of these sacred dances offers the potential for transcendence.

The Mandala

One of the tantric visual aids for meditative practice is the *mandala*, which means "circle," but actually represents a sacred universe. Through a series of concentric circles and/or squares, it details the abode, or palace, and retinue surrounding a deity. As mentioned before, in many tantric meditations the practitioner harnesses the imagination to take on the form of the deity and its enlightened qualities. Part of this process involves visualizing and navigating the royal architecture and environment of the deity—its mandala.

Some mandala representations are two-dimensional paintings that are simply blueprints of the godly abodes. Others are sculptures, models, or huge temple complexes designed as three-dimensional replicas of the divine architecture. "To be effective, and meaningful, the dance must be seen as a mandala," writes Khenpo Phuntshok Tashi, director of the National Museum of Bhutan, in *Invoking Happiness*, his colorful guide to the tshechus of Bhutan.[10] The cham function on different levels for various segments of the population.

For everyone, they serve as an anchor focusing the public's thoughts on Buddhist images, history, and values. On another level, the structure of the tantric cham echoes the formal structure of a painted mandala. The dancers, frequently led by the incense carrier and two monk musicians playing the oboes, enter the performing area (usually a large, stone courtyard of a monastery or temple) and circumambulate clockwise, creating the form of a sacred mandala, sealing the boundaries to keep out hostile forces and empowering the circumscribed space.[11] The subsequent positioning of the dancers within the performance space replicates the deities' positions in a mandala diagram.

FIGURE 12: Cham Mandala (Trongsa)

Many steps and arm movements manipulating handheld ritual implements replicate the iconography used in the two-dimensional painted renditions. The dance steps have corresponding names and functions to the symbols in the artwork and they are performed for their ascribed metaphysical powers. For example, the "thunderbolt step" is performed to cleanse and protect the sacred space from harmful powers just as in the painted mandala, the bordering ring of vajras seals the mandala universe against negative forces. In the cham, the foundations of the earth are blessed with a pair of "crossed thunderbolt

FIGURE 13: Sand Mandala (Asia Society, New York)

FIGURE 14: Monk musicians and incense carrier circumambulate the dance space clockwise initiating the outer mandala boundary. (Punakha Tshechu)

steps" in the same fashion as the blueprint for the painted version is formed on the imperturbable foundation of a crossed vajra (also a prominent feature of the national emblem of Bhutan). The action of drawing an eight-spoke wheel blesses the sphere above. The middle sphere is blessed by motioning the eight auspicious signs of Buddhism (conch, precious umbrella, victory banner, golden fish, Wheel of Dharma, endless knot, lotus, and treasure vase). Blessing the lower sphere is accomplished by outlining an eight-petal lotus below.[12]

This multidimensional, danced cosmology is further extended into the sonic realm with the addition of an acoustic mandala generated through mantra recitation and music played on the sacred instruments. According to ethnomusicologist Terry Ellingson, "Mantras may simply be described as evocative syllables and syllable sequences with ritual significance, pronounced to evoke an extraordinary state of conscious receptiveness to the generation of deities or divine qualities." Mantra vocalization works in concert with the instrumental sounds to form a sonic mandala. Ellingson further explains, "The visual mandala's characteristics of geometrical symmetry and directional orientation of line and space are transformed into sequential arrangements of musical events."[13] In other words, the musical sounds are organized to form a mandala as well.

Thus, the dance and the music enact and support the elaborate creative meditations that make up tantric Buddhist ritual. In addition, detailed visualizations are part of the cham. For example, in some cham, the dancers visualize a vajra scepter on the soles of their feet transforming and purifying the dance ground for the construction of the mandala.[14] All of these ritual actions are designed to transform the body, speech, and mind of the practitioner into a compassionate, enlightened being—a buddha. And just as in the conclusion of a sand mandala ritual, in which the mandala is dismantled and the sand grains are poured into the river as a reminder of the impermanence of all things, the cham mandala dissolves. The dancers position themselves in a final mandalic floor design before exiting with a purposeful movement phrase, one by one across the sacred space—until it is again empty.

CHAPTER FIVE

Lessons in Dance and Happiness

INSIDE RAPA

WHEN I arrived at the RAPA headquarters in the capital city of Thimphu, the vice principal, Tshering, met me in the parking lot. We walked past the outdoor courtyard, where much of the dance practice and rehearsals take place, and into RAPA's cavernous studio space with a small auditorium stage at one end. As we waited for the folk dance instructor to arrive, Tshering gave me a brief history of the academy.

Before the 1616 arrival from Tibet of Bhutan's founder Zhabdrung Ngawang Namgyal, the lamas and monastic communities were the custodians of Bhutan's sacred dances. With the early efforts to unify the country in 1625–1626 under Zhabdrung's vision and leadership, a court culture was developed, which included the performance of sacred dances in religious ceremonies as part of the state religion (*Drukpa Kagyu* lineage). The lamas and monasteries still maintained the practice of monks' cham, but as the distinct national and court culture of Bhutan evolved, a unit of all-purpose court attendants called *boegarp* (courtiers) performed various folk forms as they traveled on court business. These court attendants were also responsible for performing the lay masked dances (*boecham*) at religious ceremonies.

Fast forward to 1954, the third king, Jigme Dorji Wangchuck (1928–1972), established an institution outside of the royal court to carry on the dance traditions and provide formal training for these lay masked dances. The institution formally became RAPA in 1967. As the third king worked to develop the country and open it to the outside world, the boecham were presented for events other than just religious occasions. In keeping with its mandate to preserve the traditional songs and dances of Bhutan, RAPA added folk dance and folk music to its curriculum in 1970. The third king was also responsible for the addition of folk songs and dances to the tshechu programming. Now it is common practice to alternate folk songs with sacred dances within the tshechu lineup, creating a more diverse program and entertaining atmosphere.

Today, RAPA continues to offer three separate disciplines of study—masked dance (formerly called boecham), folk dance, and traditional music. The masked dance students are, of course, male because the dances are part of the sacred cham repertoire. By the end of the four-year program, they must perfect 31 cham, some of which last more than two hours. Folk dance majors are expected to sing the songs that accompany the dances, and they must show proficiency in 241 dances and songs. The music majors study the four traditional (non-ritual) Bhutanese instruments—*lim* (bamboo flute), *piwang* (two-string fiddle), *yangchen* (hammered dulcimer), and *dramnyen* (Bhutanese seven-stringed lute). Admission to the academy is granted through a selective process that involves a written exam and audition. The students do not pay tuition fees as the RAPA faculty members are civil servants and paid by the government. Housing in the dormitories is also subsidized by the government, leaving the students responsible for just their transportation, food, and living expenses.

The Folk Forms

My folk dance lessons were taught by Tshering Dorji, RAPA's and the nation's folk dance choreographer, a stocky, young Bhutanese man with the grace of a gazelle and the patience of a saint. He always arrived formally attired in his gho, knee socks, and very fine dress shoes. We were joined by two musicians, who enveloped us with the mystical, silvery sounds they played live on the yangchen and dramnyen to accompany the dances. Each session was an intense three to four hours during which Tshering Dorji taught me dances while he sang the accompanying folk songs, the musicians played, and the vice principal translated and made clarifications. The daily break for "tea-and-biscuits" was a welcome respite for asking questions, catching up on dance notations, and processing the flood of information.

We began with a sampling from three folk song forms that can be danced—*zhungdra*, *boedra*, and *zhey*. (There are other folk song categories that are purely vocal and not danced, and numerous local folk dance traditions that are specific to local communities.) I learned a meditative *zhungdra* (classical form from the central valleys of Bhutan) about the Black-Neck Crane (*Thrung Thrung Karmo*), a rare and endangered bird that features in much Bhutanese folklore and culture.

These beautiful birds winter in the Phobjhika Valley in Bhutan where they are studied, monitored, and protected by the Royal Society for the Protection of Nature (RSPN). The Bhutanese believe these are sacred creatures that perform traditional circumambulations of the Phobjhika Valley's famous Gangtey Gompa Monastery as they take flight and leave in the spring. Of course, there is the scientific explanation for their circling the valley: to gain the necessary altitude for clearing the high mountains as they fly north. The RSPN helped to institute a festival, celebrating these birds, that provides a forum to educate the community and visitors about the protection of nature and the environment and develops ecotourism opportunities for the locals.

The dance is simple—only three steps. The arms are extended sideways as if gliding and then they move in a fluttering motion repeated many times. The hypnotic tune has no rhythm and features a continuous melody. RAPA determined that the song was composed about 200 years ago by the second Pedtsheling Trulku (see chapter 2) as he observed the birds prancing in a meadow. Tshering Dorji then demonstrated a boedra (court dance) by the same name. That dance, by contrast, was more complicated, with many sections of rhythmic steps and gestures that move through space.

Although zhey are dances traditionally performed by men, Tshering Dorji was perfectly happy to teach one to me. After watching his demonstration of each of the four zhey, I chose to tackle *Nub Zhey*, which originated in the town of Trongsa and is performed at their tshechu. The dance starts as a slow, stately processional and then gradually increases energy, speed, and complexity in a vigorous display of squatting, clapping, turning, and jumping.

Text continues on page 50 ▸

Zhungdra

According to Bhutanese scholars, zhungdra is the oldest of the traditional Bhutanese folk forms. The songs and dances were first performed in the 17th century as a gesture of appreciation to the protective deities in gratitude for victories over Tibetan invaders. The continuous, fluid line of sound is produced using extended vocal tones in complex patterns. In an expression of worship and respect, zhungdra is usually performed by women, who stand in a horizontal line facing the lama or shrine. The singer-dancers connect by intertwining pinky fingers and perform slow, sedate, coordinated movements together with the music. See an example at https://digitalcollections.nypl.org/items/a1a61f80-e50f-0130-14e0-3c075448cc4b.

FIGURE 15: Local volunteers perform a zhungdra at the Punakha Tshechu.

Zhey

The zhey are regional expressions of praise and spirituality identified with the coming of Zhabdrung Ngawang Namgyal, the Tibetan reincarnated lama who came to Bhutan in 1616 and is credited with unifying the country while defeating Tibetan invaders. The songs typically have many verses/steps, each with a specific dedication. They alternate slow and fast rhythms and are sung and danced by men, in specified regional costumes, during their local festivals.

There are four main zhey from the four districts of

FIGURES 16: *Wang Zhey* performed at the Punakha Tshechu

the country: *Wang Zhey* from Thimphu, *Nub Zhey* from Trongsa, *Wochubi Zhey* from Paro, and *Goen Zhey* from Gasa. They all derive from the Goen Zhey. Its first known performance was by the local people of Gasa in 1616 when Zhabdrung Ngawang Namgyal escaped from Tibet and was met and welcomed in this northern region of Bhutan with this danced tribute. It is perhaps the longest Bhutanese folk dance in that it has more than 20 sections of intricate steps and is performed over the course of two days during the Gasa Tshechu. This elaborate zhey requires 21 dancers wearing costumes of pazap warriors (Zhabdrung's armed monks). The men wear a special form of wreath on their heads, acknowledging respect for the lama (Zhabdrung). Every

aspect of the costume links the dance symbolically to its religious origins among Zhabdrung's disciples.

There are also minor zhey that are more localized traditions. Some zhey originated as militia training exercises introduced by Zhabdrung's commanders. It is useful to remember that Zhabdrung himself was not only a military leader who unified the country, but also a reincarnate lama, renowned for his performances of sacred tantric cham and as a composer of song and dance. The evolution of zhey is an interesting instance where the music and dance have passed from a religious tradition into a folk custom. See the *Wang Zhey* at https://digitalcollections.nypl.org/items /0834a000-e50d-0130-3a3e-3c075448cc4b.

Boedra

Boedra (court form) means "melody of the court attendants" and is believed to have been developed, later than the other two forms, by the attendants who served the king as they traveled on official assignments. Boedra are faster songs with a metered rhythm. The use of a five-tone, or pentatonic, scale gives all of these folk forms a minor, mystical mood. See the boedra *Thrung Thrung Karmo* at https://digitalcollections.nypl.org/items/005ac760-f877-0130-341e-3c075448cc4b.

FIGURE 17: A boedra performed by RAPA dancers at the Punakha Tshechu

A presentation of zhey was featured at the royal wedding of the popular fifth king. Because Bhutan is a culture that reveres and ennobles those who perform the dances, the honored bridegroom also learned a zhey, from my instructor Tshering Dorji (the nation's folk dance choreographer), to perform before the public.

Tshering Dorji made it quite clear that the zhungdra and zhey are unalterable dances "like cham." However, new boedra are currently composed. The *Je Khenpo* (highest religious official in the country) is a noted composer of boedra that, along with choreography set by the national choreographer at RAPA, are frequently performed at the sacred festivals. This culture, full of so much immutable tradition derived from dreams, visions, and history, still allows itself room to grow and renew.

I learned to dance a 300-year-old boedra, *Zampa la Mitsuk*, about constructing a holy bridge (left, see translated lyrics). The pleasing, simple tune was easy enough to reproduce and the dance steps flowed rhythmically. An initial walking pattern was followed by sections of stomping and touching the heel forward and a brief kneel onto one knee on the ground.

I also opted to learn a more recently composed boedra that I had seen performed at the Paro Tshechu. I was able to make this request by demonstrating a few of the defining arm and hand gestures. Tshering Dorji really did not speak any English beyond, "Left, right, one-two-three," and I did not speak any *Dzongkha* (official language of Bhutan) beyond the greeting "Kuzuzampo la." This boedra, *Choden Mengoen* (Religious Country), was choreographed by Tshering Dorji to a tune composed by RAPA students. Though it appeared to be simple enough with graceful and interesting gestures, the dance was actually quite complex, with very little or no repetition and continually changing floor patterns. At one point, to overcome the language barrier and my confusion over the spatial formations, Tshering Dorji took a piece of chalk and drew a circle on the floor; then he demonstrated the dancer's constantly changing relationship to the circular floor plan.

Zampa la Mitsuk (LYRICS)

I am going to build a bridge—
   a golden bridge for the high
   lamas to use in crossing.
I am going to build a bridge—
   a silver bridge for the king and
   high officials to use in crossing.
I am going to build a bridge—
   a bronze bridge for our beloved
   father to use in crossing.

The men's legwork is more energetic and interesting than the women's—probably because women are constrained by wearing the *kira*, the traditional straight, floor-length, tightly wrapped skirt. The steps continuously flow with the only complication being that frequently the foot is placed on the floor without bearing any weight. I was never really sure whether to tap or stand on my foot. Hand gestures are quite intricate, and finger placement is precise. Fingers are held relaxed but together, and hand gestures incorporate frequent wrist rotations as the fingers transition from this relaxed position to holding the thumb to the middle finger one-third down from the tip. The academy artists explained that the hands and arms frequently press down or away from the body, which represents pressing away evil and negativity. When palms are facing upward with arms extending to the front or sides, it represents offering or supplication.

In Bhutan, Everyone Is a Dancer

Each night, using the video recording my husband was making during the sessions along with the detailed notes I had taken, I practiced the material from the day's dance lesson. As I viewed the videos, I perceived a difference between the way my instructor held his fingers and my own attempts, but correcting it was eluding me.

Then one day when we were driving along the one and only highway that crosses the entire length of the country from west to east, our driver had to stop at a road block that would not open for 25 minutes. Road widening, repair, and clearing landslides are constants along this single highway that crosses this mountainous country. Bhutanese travelers are quite accustomed to long waits at road blocks and even posted hours for passage at particular areas. We got out of our van to stretch our legs, and I decided to use the time to practice the dance I had just learned. All of a sudden, the middle-aged driver Dawa came running over to correct my hand and finger positions. He was quite emphatic and precise about my finger placement. His intervention was invaluable; he had pinpointed the discrepancy and explained how to rectify it. Who knew our driver was such an expert? But I eventually realized that everyone in Bhutan is a dancer—from the Buddhist master, Guru Rinpoche, to Zhabdrung Ngawang Namgyal, the brilliant military leader; from the popular fifth king, Jigme Khesar Namgyel, to my driver, Dawa.

I saw another example of this when we visited a middle school. Schools in Bhutan are frequently boarding schools, because many children must travel from faraway farm villages. It was "back-to-school week," and the students had just returned from their winter vacation. Classes had not yet begun, and the entire country was eagerly preparing for the king's birthday celebration, which is a national holiday. Groups of students were rehearsing all over the campus. Boys belted out the folk songs as they energetically performed their dances; girls were dancing as they sang or practicing to recorded music; coed groups went through their paces in a fun-yet-purposeful manner—all unsupervised (and these were middle school students, around 13 years old).

The next day we attended the national celebration of the king's birthday held in the stadium in Thimphu. Student dancers from the country's high schools performed for government officials, the assembled spectators, and (via television) the entire nation. I climbed the bleacher steps and sat next to a group of high school girls dressed in their school uniforms (kiras and same-colored jackets) fresh out of their morning classes. I glanced at the notebooks in their laps and asked if I could take a peak. There, in the notes from that day's economics lesson, was an explanation of the formula for GNH compared with the formula for GDP.

The final dance presentation ended with the dancers forming the letters GNH in the center of the stadium. Afterward, they invited the entire audience onto the field to participate in the closing ceremonial dance, *Tashi Leybey*. The stadium was flooded with participants—old and young, government officials and regular folk. In the typical conclusion to all Bhutanese social events, they danced together and sang, soliciting divine blessings for long life, prosperity, and of course—happiness.

FIGURE 18: *Tashi Leybey* concludes a National Day celebration in Thimphu's Changlimithang Stadium.

PART III:
Deeper into the Dance Culture

CHAPTER SIX

Punakha! From War to Enlightenment

IRETURNED FOR my third journey to the country to deepen my understanding of the world of cham—the sacred dances of Himalayan Buddhism that are practiced as a means to spiritual transformation. In particular I wanted the practitioners' perspective, which I hoped to obtain through a series of interviews. So, I returned to this hidden land, tucked into the folds of the mountains and valleys of the Himalayas, where the people transmit their values and beliefs through movement—a society that holds its dance as sacred and powerful.

I arranged to attend the Punakha Tshechu and the final day of the *drubchen* that precedes it. "Drubchen" means "great accomplishment" and is an 8–10-day period of continuous, intensive ceremonial practice that is often held before a tshechu.

The trip requires two days of plane flights and four hours of travel by car along steep, winding mountain roads into the warm, verdant, terraced valley of Punakha. The Punakha Tshechu and Drubchen are dedicated to the memory of Zhabdrung Ngawang Namgyal, the unifier and first ruler of the nation of Bhutan. In addition to all of the usual features of a tshechu and drubchen, the Punakha Tshechu and Drubchen contain specific rituals and programming that commemorate and honor Bhutan's founding father and is, therefore, a unique and hugely significant event.

THE NARROW ESCAPE OF ZHABDRUNG NGAWANG NAMGYAL

In 1616, the Tibetan lama Ngawang Namgyal barely escaped from Tibet with his life. His entitlement to the throne of the Drukpa Kagyu sect of Tibetan

Buddhism was being challenged by a rival contender. The claim to leadership, and to the honorific title of Gwalyang Drukpa, rested on being recognized as the current reincarnation of Pema Karpo (1527-1592) the great scholar and prince-abbot of Ralung Monastery (headquarters of the order). Ngawang Namgyal, a descendant of the founder of the lineage Tsangpa Gyare (1161–1211), had been recognized and groomed from childhood for this role. At the age of eight he had already been given the title of *zhabdrung*, which means "at whose feet one submits."

The powerful Tsang ruler of Tibet favored the rival candidate and sent armed soldiers with a warrant for Ngawang Namgyal's arrest. The lama fled to Bhutan, having received a vision, in a dream, that the guardian deities invited him to seek refuge there. In what proved to be a provocative act, he took with him the *Rangjung Kharsapani*, a precious relic believed to have emerged from a vertebra in the cremated remains of Tsangpa Gyare. Ngawang Namgyal entered Bhutan through the northern region of Laya and was welcomed with a local folk dance, *Goen Zhey*, performed in his honor. In the years that followed, however, Tibetan forces repeatedly invaded Bhutan in their determination to retrieve the venerated relic, which was supposed to be held by the rightful leader of the lineage.

In Bhutan, Ngawang Namgyal is simply known as the Zhabdrung. He is credited with establishing the Drukpa Kagyu order as the principal school of Buddhism in Bhutan (Kagyu being one of the main lineages of Himalayan Buddhism). He is also credited with unifying and founding the Bhutanese state and with instituting a dual system of government (secular and religious). Among his celebrated feats was using a ruse to repel a 1639 Tibetan invasion of the Punakha Valley, where he was in residence and holding the relic. The large Tibetan force camped in the fields alongside the Mo Chu (Mother River), readying to attack. The Zhabdrung and his outnumbered local militia, the *pazap*, were stationed inside the valley's great fortress and monastery, the Punakha Dzong. But the Zhabdrung devised a stratagem that tricked the Tibetans into retreating empty-handed. Zhabdrung Ngawang Namgyal marked the triumph by introducing the Punakha Drubchen, an annual period of rituals and sacred dances appeasing Yeshey Goenpo, also known as Mahakala, one of the main protector deities of Bhutan.

The Punakha Drubchen

In commemoration of their transformative victory over the Tibetans, every year the Je Khenpo, Bhutan's head abbot and spiritual leader, and the Central Monastic Body, comprising more than 250 monks, hold the Punakha Drubchen in which they perform private religious ceremonies for several days inside the temple of the Punakha Dzong. These include constructing a mandala from sand, artifacts, and relics; prayers; and performing sacred dances as an expression of gratitude to the nation's guardian deities. The final day, which falls on the ninth day of the first month of Bhutan's lunar calendar (usually in late February), is a public occasion in which designated members of the community dress up as warriors to reenact the historic battle. On the climactic last day, outfitted in their finest ceremonial apparel as they would to attend a tshechu, the villagers from the Punakha district gather to observe the events.

FIGURE 19: The Punakha Dzong (Palace of Great Bliss) sits beside the Mo Chu.

THE REENACTMENT

People make their way across the covered wooden bridge that spans the Mo Chu, entering the grounds of the Punakha Dzong. As I approach the entrance to the massive structure (also known as The Palace of Great Bliss), three village men dressed up as warriors are dancing at the top of the dzong's wooden stairway, originally designed to be lifted up in times of war and make the fortress impregnable to invaders. They chant and dance while two men continuously pull the thick ropes that ring the two dzong bells. Others set off firecrackers and shout war cries, filling the air with the sounds, smoke, and smell of gunpowder and warfare. Their dance (called *Beh*) is derived from a martial drill and training sequence. The simple steps, followed by a turn, with a fist raised, signal that the war games have commenced.

These warrior/dancers, 136 in all, are dressed up in black-and-red battle gear, some with metal helmets decorated with flags, and are equipped with iron swords and shields as well as bows and arrows. They represent the pazap militia, the group of peasant warriors that Zhabdrung Ngawang Namgyal could call up on short notice, since the fledgling nation could not afford a standing army. As in earlier times, today they are men from the *Wang Tshogchen Gyed*, the eight great clans of the region between Thimphu (the capital city, some 50 miles to the southwest) and Punakha. Each clan sends 17 people to participate: 14 warriors, one cook, one head warrior (general), and one village headman. These symbolic regiments have been camping out together in the vicinity, practicing for two weeks prior to participating in the drubchen rituals and the final day's reenactment.

The spectators enter the dzong by the staircase and gradually assemble in the courtyard. Each contingent of soldiers performs the dance on the staircase and then enters the courtyard. After several groups of

---

 Beh

According to Core of Culture's Bhutan Dance Project, "The Beh dances were introduced by the Zhabdrung after the victory over the Tibetan forces in 1639."[15] As the men chant their war song, they balance—first on one leg (rising up on the ball of the foot several times) and then the other—in a display of mind/body strength and control. In other versions of the dance, usually performed on a level surface (as opposed to a steep staircase), I have seen the one-legged balances replaced with repeated one-legged hops. Each of the eight great clans has its own lyrics to the war chant. See it for yourself at https://digitalcollections.nypl.org/items/ffcad140-e7ef-0130-c08a-3c075448cc4b.

soldiers have gathered in the courtyard, they form a circle for a *zhey*, a dance of praise and spirituality that is identified with the coming of the Zhabdrung. Their chanting voices grow louder, gathering volume as additional soldiers keep arriving to join the circle. The leader chants a verse and the entire group responds in chant. Performing the 21 sections of this men's ceremonial dance, these villagers, old and young, chant and move as one.

A group of little, red-robed monk novices comes skipping through the entranceway to join the action. The warriors gather into a tighter circle,

FIGURE 20: Pazap reenactors dance a zhey in the courtyard of Punakha Dzong.

holding pinky fingers. They sway side to side while their arms swing easily up and down. The tempo starts slowly, then gradually builds.

Various ministers of Parliament start to arrive, easily identified by their special colored *kabney* (ceremonial sashes). Looking very official, they stand outside the circle of dancers, conversing with the head monks. The courtyard becomes filled with spectators as everyone waits for the Je Khenpo, who will officiate at the *Nub Chu Sha* (Casting of the Relic ceremony), commemorating Zhabdrung Ngawang Namgyal's ingenious battle strategy.

All eyes are trained on the courtyard balcony as the district officials enter and take their places, followed by the yellow-robed Je Khenpo and his assistant head monks. The Je Khenpo takes his seat on his central, yellow satin throne. The pazap warriors, chanting and swaying in a stationary dance and linking pinkies or at times performing hand gestures, turn to face their spiritual leader in three tight lines stretching across the width of the courtyard.

The pazaps then form two rows facing each other for the *marchang* (libation offering) ceremony. *Chang* is a Bhutanese alcoholic brew that is collected for the event from every family in the community and displayed in the courtyard in a vast, decorated metal urn. The marchang offering is a significant tantric Buddhist practice performed to enhance and sacralize an event. The chang will be offered to the deity Mahakala to invoke protection and benefits for the community for the coming year. It is believed that each and every Bhutanese is guarded by Mahakala. This deity of Indian origin was absorbed into the pantheon of tantric deities and is considered a fierce protector of the Buddhist path, or *dharma*.

In turn, each of the eight headmen performs *Lemah*, a solo dance and chant before the Je Khenpo (see description on opposite page).

Afterward, the marchang ritual, performed by the pazap soldiers, head monks, and Je Khenpo, continues inside the temple.

The Ruse

Meanwhile, the crowd starts moving out of the great doorway of the dzong to find places on the outer grounds in order to watch the next act. (This is an

Lemah

Lemah is a dance particular to the Punakha Drubchen in that it contains an accounting of the payment of taxes to the government that was required of each clan before the Punakha Drubchen could commence. Punakha was Zhabdrung's "seat" or headquarters. The dance has all the excitement of an accountant detailing a tax payment as each of the eight clan headmen repeats the quiet, deliberate steps. Moving forward through the two rows of soldiers toward the giant urn, the dancer first bows, then points his bow and arrow to the four directions. He proceeds forward and backward with a series of carefully placed steps, intoning a narrative chant in praise of his particular clan deities and recounting details pertaining to his clan's district:

> *It is an auspicious time here, and everything is as it should be. We have come to Punakha, together with our deity, . . . to participate in the Drubchen. Last year we had a wonderful time at the Drubchen, and this year we will do the same, at this time of the auspicious waxing energies of the first part of the month.*
>
> From the Bhutan Dance Project[16]

event in which the public follows the performers from location to location to observe the reenactment of the historical event in its exact geography.) Everyone is now sitting or standing in anticipation. Some horses, having been brought and saddled, are ready and waiting. Two monks start the steady chime of the dzong bells. The pazap warriors chant and dance the martial *Beh* once again on the grand stairway, this time wielding swords in their raised fists. They sing,

> *When Mahakala becomes incensed with anger, he turns into the wrathful Raven-Headed Mahakala, and then he roars like a thunder-dragon; that is, when his shouting voice most protects the Buddhism of Bhutan. All evil spirits are vanquished. . . . Beware!*
>
> From the Bhutan Dance Database

The wrathful lyrics conclude with a fierce war cry as the pazap warriors descend the great stairway. This goes on for what feels like forever—which indeed reenacts the Zhabdrung's strategy. The pazap fighters performing the dance move down the stairway, then run around the back of the dzong to perform it over and over again, emulating the undersize Bhutanese militia that repeatedly marched out of the dzong, circled around to the rear, and reentered through a hidden back door to emerge again. Thus they fooled the Tibetan soldiers, lying in wait across the Mo Chu, into fearing that the Bhutanese had many more troops than they actually did.

FIGURE 21: Pazap reenactors dancing the martial *Beh* dance

The dance is finally concluded and a general, in a white-skirted costume with a tall, fringed, wine-colored hat, descends the stairway, mounts a waiting horse, and is paraded around the central flagpole by his men, who carry a multicolored victory banner above his head. Afterward, his men lead him and his horse down to the bank of the river. The other generals repeat this dramatic exit.

PROCESSION AND CASTING OF THE RELIC

When the final pazap contingent has left the dzong grounds and crossed the wooden bridge to the opposite side of the Mo Chu (where the Tibetans had been camped), the entire monastic body parades in formal procession down the grand stairway and out of the dzong grounds and assembles along the near bank of the Mo Chu. This climactic scene is a rainbow of color, as the monks wear their ceremonial red hats and carry colorful pendants, banners, flags, and *torma* (ritual offerings of flour and butter sculpted into intricate, multicolored forms). The monk musicians wear robes of vibrant hues in silk brocade and play drums, cymbals, conch shells, and trumpets, filling the air with sounds of ceremony. The entire community follows the procession and then splits, depending on which side of the river they want to view the event from.

The main actor is the Je Khenpo, who performs the Casting of the Relic ceremony, which Zhabdrung Ngawang Namgyal initially performed. It reenacts the legendary action that capped the

FIGURE 22: A general on horseback is paraded to the banks of the Mo Chu.

triumph over the Tibetan forces. The Je Khenpo is dressed in the costume of a Black Hat master—also worn by the Zhabdrung in some artistic depictions. Its distinguishing wide-brim, round black hat is strapped to his head and topped with a mirror, skull figure, and peacock feathers—each element full of symbolic meaning. Over his black robe is an apron adorned with the electrifying and wrathful face of Mahakala. This costume, assimilated from that of pre-Buddhist magician-priests, is worn by accomplished masters of tantric Buddhism in esoteric practices for which Zhabdrung Ngawang Namgyal was renowned.

FIGURE 23: Monks exit the Punakha Dzong blowing trumpets.

The Je Khenpo, accompanied by a monk carrying a resplendent parasol to shelter him, is at the center of the procession. They stop at a certain point by the river where the Zhabdrung performed this same ritual in the 17th century. A monk prepares a silver goblet with offerings—sands collected from the mandala that had been constructed as part of the drubchen rituals inside the temple. The Je Khenpo pours them into the flowing water.

Several underwear-clad young men have taken up positions in the river. They say the water is freezing at this time of year. In the grand finale of this historical reenactment, the Je Khenpo tosses a basketful of oranges, one

FIGURE 24: Monks exit the Punakha Dzong in procession with ceremonial banners.

FIGURE 25: Je Khenpo heads toward the Mo Chu wearing the Black Hat costume.

by one, into the river. They symbolize the substitute relic that the Zhabdrung cast into the Mo Chu, tricking the Tibetans into believing the sought-after Rangjung Kharsapani had been thrown into the river and lost forever in the current. With their morale already dampened by thinking themselves outnumbered, and then having no hope of securing the relic, the Tibetan warriors retreated.

Not discouraged on this day are the hardy Bhutanese swimmers, who quickly cut through the icy cold waters and pounce on the orange orbs, believed to bring blessings for the coming year. One successful swimmer makes his way to his happy family waiting on shore and is rewarded for his efforts with *doma* (betel nut and lime paste wrapped in a banana leaf). The Bhutanese love to chew this preparation, which makes teeth and lips an orange-red.

The monks' procession returns to the dzong, as do the pazap contingents. In a final dramatic flourish, led by their soldiers, the generals on horseback circle the flagpole. At the base of the great stairway leading into the dzong, the soldiers hoist the generals off their horses and carry them aloft—up the stairs and into the courtyard for celebrations.

Rehearsal for the Tshechu

Later that afternoon, back in the courtyard of the dzong, rehearsals are under-way for the tshechu that will begin the next day. A few onlookers sit under the magnificent *bodhi* tree as gentle breezes blow through the leaves. This tree is said to have been propagated from the fig tree (*ficus*) under which the Buddha sat until he attained enlightenment. Large painted backdrops for a modern production dramatizing the coming of the Zhabdrung to Bhutan are being hung. A huge throne for the Zhabdrung character is moved into place by pazap reenactors who performed dances and rituals all morning. Now they are stagehands moving props for the next day's events.

Local residents who volunteered to perform in the tshechu are rehearsing a famous dance-drama, *Shawa Shachi Cham* (The Dance of the Stag and the Hounds). In this culture that transmits its history, values, and beliefs through dance, the volunteers will be performing the story of the beloved saint and yogi from the 11th century, Milarepa, who converts a merciless animal hunter to the Buddhist view of respecting all life as interdependent. Only a few hours ago this courtyard was filled with war cries and gun smoke, and now Punakha continues the journey from war to enlightenment—all of it danced, of course.

CHAPTER SEVEN

Behind the Sacred Mask:
The Abbot, the Farmer, the Mother, and the Monk

To begin to understand the experience of the practitioners, I arranged to meet Khenpo Phuntshok Tashi, Director of the National Museum of Bhutan, and the author of *Invoking Happiness: Guide to the Sacred Festivals of Bhutan and Gross National Happiness*. He had performed the cham himself from the time he was a 12-year-old monk, and he is an expert on the subject.

Meeting the Khenpo

In Bhutan it is customary to present a person of stature, or a guest, with a *khata*, a ceremonial long white scarf, as a sign of respect. I guessed there would be a prescribed protocol for presenting the khata, so I asked my new guide, Ugyen, to teach me, and was astonished by the detail involved. Ugyen showed me how to gather the fabric into accordion folds and hold it just so until the moment of presentation. Then with a choreographed courtly flourish, you toss open the khata and catch it on the forearms, palms uplifted, presenting it to the recipient. Attending Bhutanese etiquette class from the age of seven, Ugyen had learned this in school. It is one of the customs in the Bhutanese code of behavior (*driglam namzha*) instituted by Zhabdrung Ngawang Namgyal.

When I met the *khenpo* (a religious title meaning "abbot") outside my hotel entrance, I did my best to perform the khata presentation with grace. However, nothing could equal the graciousness of Khenpo Tashi when he received the khata and then placed it around my neck. (He has since told me, with a chuckle, that at the time he wondered why this crazy, Western woman wanted to meet with him to talk about cham. But we are now good friends and communicate regularly.)

We proceeded down the outdoor path lined with blossoming cherry and apple trees to the hotel's meditation house—a square, natural-wood-paneled room bathed in sunshine through the wall of windows. There we conversed for two hours about the history, practice, and even politics of cham in Bhutan.

The Dancing Guru

From the historical myths, it becomes apparent that the documentation of cham, like much of the early history of the region, hovers between fact and wondrous legend. For example, the key actor in disseminating cham was the tantric master, Guru Rinpoche, who is said to have been born of a lotus flower in the center of a lake in the northwestern Indian kingdom of Oddiyana, in what is now the Swat Valley of Pakistan. His renown as an accomplished tantric practitioner led to demand for his spiritual assistance across the Himalayas. The Bhutanese and Tibetans may dispute the order of events, but it is generally agreed that they occurred sometime in the middle of the eighth century. There are accounts of his invitation and visit to Bumthang (in Bhutan) to come to the aid of the dying king, Sindhu Raja. The stories abound of how Guru Rinpoche marshaled supernatural powers through meditation and performing cham, thereby curing the king, converting him to Buddhism, and transforming the local deity (who had sickened the king) into a guardian of Buddhism.

The stories continue that while meditating in a cave in Nepal, Guru Rinpoche was bidden by Tibetan King Trisong Deutsen to come and help defeat the "local deities" who were hindering the construction of the first Buddhist monastery in Tibet at Samye. (It was eventually completed around 779 C.E.) The non-Buddhist priests and shamans (the entrenched religious power structure) were the more likely culprits who were obstructing the project. The story is told that upon his arrival, the Guru performed the *Vajrakilaya* cham through which he captivated, subdued, and converted the opposing spirits to become protectors of Buddhism.

FIGURE 26: Taktsang (Tiger's Nest)

The accounts go on to tell of more visits to Bhutan—the most famous being his flight on the back of a tigress to the cave at *Taktsang*, or Tiger's Nest, that hugs the side of a perilous cliff in the Paro valley. In fact, no visit to Bhutan is complete without making the mind-blowing pilgrimage along the winding mountain path, across the steep ravine beside a crashing waterfall, and up the endless stairs to the Taktsang temple complex, which clings to the granite ledges of a cliff. I consider it to be the ninth wonder of the world. It is told that the Guru took on the appearance of the wrathful deity, *Dorje Drolöd* (Wild,

Wrathful Vajra), while his Bhutanese consort, Tashi Kheudren, transformed herself into a tigress. They flew together to Taktsang subduing the region's obstructive forces to make way for the teachings of Buddhism.

The Dancing Guru's Dance

The miraculous activities of Guru Rinpoche are enumerated in one of the most sacred and anticipated dances of the tshechu—*Guru Tshengye Cham* (The Eight Names of the Guru or Eight Manifestations; see pages 76–87). This two-hour cham catalogs the Guru's eight forms, which he manifested to meet the demands of the moment—like a spiritual super-hero. The eight manifestations rendered in *Guru Tshengye Cham* are his most famous forms; many more have been identified in more than two dozen sacred biographies. It is believed that through his numerous manifestations, Guru Rinpoche was able to benefit all sentient beings.

Dance Power

Scholars trace the origins of cham to Indian tantric ritual and pre-Buddhist Tibetan folk religion. Since ancient times, dance has been an important element of Tibetan religious ritual. During pre-Buddhist times, to keep the cosmic and social order intact, rulers, upon assuming power, would perform a ritual dance to procure the supernatural force from the previous ruler.[17] As Buddhism spread throughout Asia, it absorbed and incorporated many of the beliefs and rituals of the indigenous peoples of each locale. The story of Guru Rinpoche's conversion of unfriendly and obstructive non-Buddhist deities into protectors, or guardian deities, of Buddhism by performing dance rituals co-opted from their own repertoire is a wonderful illustration of this. The pacification and conversion of these pre-Buddhist local spirits by Guru Rinpoche is reenacted in and a major theme of many of the rituals and cham performed today. Actually, when Guru Rinpoche performed the seminal *Vajrakilaya Cham* at Samye, he was executing a ground purification rite *that incorporates a dance* to cleanse the site of all obstacles for the building of the monastery. This type of earth ritual involves requesting the use of the site, cleansing the site, and seizing the ground from the earth spirits and is still typically performed before the construction of a house, temple, or ritual sand mandala—or before the start of a tshechu.[18] What is noteworthy is that this oft-repeated ritual involves dance.

Khenpo Tashi explained, "There are two categories of cham dance in Bhutanese tradition. One is the dances of the gods, usually performed by monks. The other consists of the cham performed by laity." However, Khenpo Tashi emphasized, "In reality, there is no difference. All cham are considered the sacred dance of Guru Rinpoche."[19]

Cham is said to be the timeless wisdom of the buddha realm transmitted into the human world through Guru Rinpoche to his 25 disciples, and passed down for generations. Even the act of viewing cham is regarded as an opportunity for spiritual awakening, which they call *thongdrel*, meaning "liberation through seeing." The dances are all considered sacred mandalas—archetypal models of an enlightened universe.

THE DANCERS

And who are the dancers who perform this enlightened activity? All Bhutanese monks learn the monks' dances as part of the monastic curriculum. Cham instruction usually begins between the ages of 12 and 15. However, not all monks excel at or go on to perform the dances in private temple rituals or public festivals. Later the monks learn meditation practices that will eventually precede and influence their cham performance—helping them to empty their minds of their own ego and embody the qualities, both physical and spiritual, of the deities they will represent in the dances. Khenpo Tashi stressed that the emphasis in teaching the cham is on the movements (as opposed to the meditation, which comes later). To be clear, the dancers are not in a trance state, although trance is used in other dance practices (of oracles and shamans). The dancers are fully aware of and intentional in their actions. Because these dances are considered to be primordial wisdom—envisioned, recorded, danced, and taught by enlightened lamas—they are unalterable, as every aspect of the movement and the costume is imbued with significance.

Guru Tshengye Cham (THE EIGHT MANIFESTATIONS OF THE GURU)

This cham is a revealed treasure dance, or tercham, derived from the *Lama Sangdu* scriptures discovered by the great Tibetan *terton* (treasure revealer) Guru Chokyi Wangchuk, popularly known as Guru Chowang (1212–1270).

The expectant sound of droning oboes builds a sense of excitement in the crowd as the wrathful manifestation Dorje Drolöd opens the dance by taking possession of the ground with a series of ceremonial, high, marching steps crossing the dance space back and

FIGURE 27: Dorje Drolöd in *Guru Tshengye Cham* (Punakha Tshechu)

forth, with arms uplifted, holding the ritual scepter in one hand and the dagger in the other. Usually danced by the *champon* (dance master), he acts as the master of ceremonies. He goes on to lead a formal circular procession in which the fully enlightened Guru Pema Jungney (actually a ninth manifestation portrayed by a master lama who doesn't dance), dressed in his robes, golden mask, and signature five-petal hat, is paraded to his throne in grand style—with an ornamental parasol, colorful banners, incense, musicians, and a complete entourage. Meanwhile, Dorje Drolöd and the other Guru emanations, along with a retinue of wrathful deities, continue to dance in a wide circle spinning back and forth.

Eight monks take turns dancing into the center of the circle and performing solos representing each manifestation. These danced solos are not pantomimed or dramatized, but are distinguished mainly through the striking masks and costumes and less so through the choreography. The manifestations'

FIGURE 28: Procession of Pema Jungney (Punakha Tshechu)

movements are mostly differentiated by the dancers' level of energy. The peaceful manifestations dance with deliberate majesty while the wrathful manifestations dance with building energy and speed. Meanwhile, the other monks remaining in the wide circle mirror the movements of the featured manifestation and intone praises to each form of Guru Rinpoche. See for yourself at https://digitalcollections.nypl.org/items/25396c00-e7f0-0130-f1ae-3c075448cc4b.

THE EIGHT MANIFESTATIONS

❖ **Guru Tshokye Dorje** (Lake-Born Vajra) wears a blue brocade robe and peaceful blue-green mask. These colors call to mind the Guru's miraculous birth, from a lotus flower on Lake Dhanakosha in the kingdom of Oddiyana, as an eight-year-old, fully enlightened being. He was adopted by the childless King Indrabhuti and raised in the royal palace as the crown prince. He dances with a *phurba* (three-bladed ritual dagger) in one hand and a small bell in the other.

❖ **Guru Shakya Sengye** (Lion of the Shakya clan) appears dressed in a monk's robe and a peaceful golden mask that resembles the Buddha's face with his hairstyle of tight curls. He holds a monk's begging bowl in his hands like Buddha Shakyamuni. The Guru received this designation when he renounced the palace, took monastic ordination, and sought to deepen his dharma practice.

❖ **Guru Loden Chogse** (Proclaimer of Wisdom) wears a brocade robe and a peaceful ivory mask. His hair is styled in a topknot and he wears a crown. He holds a *damaru* in his right hand and a mirror in his left. The Guru was recognized in this aspect once he had mastered the *Vajrayana* (esoteric Buddhist) teachings and practiced in the sacred sites in India.

❖ **Guru Padmasambhava** (Lotus-Born) is dressed in a red and gold monk's robe and the red, pointed hat of a Buddhist scholar. He carries a skull-cup in his right hand and forms the teaching mudra with his left. This manifestation resulted from the time during which he and his spiritual consort Princess Mandarava retreated to the cave at Maratika in Nepal to perfect longevity practices. Her father, the King of Zahor, was displeased with this arrangement and sentenced them to be burned to death. All were amazed to find that Padmasambhava had transformed the pyre into a lake, and there they both sat safely on a lotus blossom!

❖ **Guru Nyima Ozer** (Sunbeam) is costumed in a golden brocade robe with a yellow-complexioned, bearded mask and carries a trident. This designation arose from his time meditating and teaching the esoteric practices in the eight cremation grounds. During this chapter the Guru developed legendary powers and performed miracles, such as causing the sun to stand still.

- ❖ **Guru Padma Gyalpo** (Lotus King) dances in a red brocade robe and orange-tinged mask while carrying a small drum and mirror in his hands. The Guru assumed this appearance when he returned to Oddiyana where evil chieftains attempted to set him on fire. Unable to burn him, they converted to Buddhism and offered their kingdom to the Guru.
- ❖ **Guru Sengye Dradog** (Lion's Roar) wears a blue brocade robe and a terrifying blue mask with four sharp fangs and a crown of five skulls. While the Guru was at Bodh Gaya, the site where the Buddha attained enlightenment, 500 non-Buddhist opponents threatened to obliterate the Buddhist doctrine. The Guru overcame their menacing threats with concentration, intellectual debate, and miraculous powers.
- ❖ **Guru Dorje Drolöd** (Wild, Wrathful Vajra)—the most wrathful emanation wears a brocade robe and terrifying dark-red mask crowned with five skulls and matted red and blue dreadlocks. He holds a phurba in one hand and a *dorje* (ritual scepter) in the other. Legends recount that assuming this form, he rode on the back of his consort-turned-tigress from Singye Dzong in the east to Taktsang (Tiger's Nest Cave) in the west and vanquished obstructive spirits, converting them to guardian protectors of Buddhism.

FIGURE 29: Guru Loden Chogse in *Guru Tshengye Cham* (Trongsa Tshechu)

FIGURE 30: Guru Padmasambhava in *Guru Tshengye Cham* (Punakha Tshechu)

FIGURE 31: Guru Nyima Ozer in *Guru Tshengye Cham* (Punakha Tshechu)

FIGURE 32: Guru Singye Dradog in *Guru Tshengye Cham* (Punakha Tshechu)

FIGURE 33: Retinue of Wrathful Deities in *Guru Tshengye Cham* (Punakha Tshechu)

FIGURE 34: (Opposite) Monks rehearse *Rigma Chudruk Cham*. (Trongsa Drong).

Rigma Chudruk Cham (Dance of the Sixteen Dakinis)

Once the eight manifestations complete their dance and exit, another cham is introduced into the larger dance—Dance of the Sixteen *Dakinis* (Feminine Wisdom Facilitators), or *Rigma Chudruk Cham*. It is a cham within the cham. In this offering dance to the Guru, 16 dancers sing and dance the presentation of pleasing gifts (flowers, incense, butter lamps, perfume, ornaments, and so on) to Guru Rinpoche.*

For this dance, young, slender monks are costumed to look like dakinis in long, brocade dresses overlaid

*Dance used for invocation and to convey offerings during worship was a customary practice in ancient India, codified in the *Vedas* (Sanskrit texts dating back to 1500 B.C.E.) and sculpted onto temple walls throughout the country. It is useful to remember that some Vajrayana liturgies and rituals were composed by Indian Buddhist teachers and are modeled on these cultural traditions.

with aprons of carved-bone latticework. These spiritual guides dance unmasked, wearing wigs of long black hair with a crown of five golden lobes—each with a symbol of one of the Five Wisdom Buddhas (five qualities of enlightenment represented as five directional, color-coded buddhas in mandalic design). Their dance movements are slow, serene, and purposeful, accompanied by continuous flowing arm motions and complex mudras that symbolize the specific offerings to the Guru. They look as if they are speaking a sign language. The dance is performed in lines that eventually coalesce into a horseshoe formation. The choreography involves rattling the damaru with the right hand to awaken all from ignorance, as the left hand performs mudras while ringing the hand bell, which signifies emptiness (of inherent identity). In the middle of the cham, the dancers stand still and chant a sacred song as one of their many gifts to Guru Rinpoche. See the cham at https://digitalcollections.nypl.org/items/29ac1bb0-e7f0-0130-67da-3c075448cc4b.

During the tshechu, while the monks are performing these dances, the entire crowd of festival attendees lines up to receive blessings and a prayer cord from the seated Guru and his attending monks. At this point, performance and real-life merge as the audience members enter the performance space to interact with the performers in their roles as enlightened beings, and the performance becomes a real-life ritual event.

As the dakinis complete their dance, the Guru's entourage of wrathful deities comes swirling into the dance space. They lead another circular procession followed by Guru Rinpoche, his eight manifestations, consorts, monks, local officials, folk dancers, the incense carrier, and the musicians. The dakinis, continuing their flowing choreography, bring up the rear as the oboes, dungchen, bells, cymbals, drums, and chanting fill the air with the sounds and sights of Vajrayana Buddhism. Through the *Guru Tshengye Cham*, the Bhutanese recreate a mandala—a vision of a perfect universe—and place themselves in it. They join in the company of their spiritual heroes as they pay homage to and seek blessings from their revered Guru.

FIGURE 35: Folk dancers, musicians, and district officials join the Guru's procession in *Guru Tshengye Cham* (Punakha Tshechu).

The Monk

While attending the Punakha Tshechu, I talked with Wangchuk, a monk dancer. He is currently a member of the Central Monastic Body, the government-supported monks under the authority of the Je Khenpo. Most of the year the monks of the Central Monastic Body live in the Thimphu Dzong located in the capital city of Thimphu, but they spend winters in the Punakha Dzong, in the town of Punakha, the winter capital of the former kingdom.

This tall, slender, 30-year-old monk, with his high chiseled cheekbones, had been the lead dancer for the famous *Zhanag Cham* (Black Hat Dance) during an earlier performance. I had been transfixed by his dancing during the entire 40-minute ground purification ritual. The monk dancers wear colored silk-brocade robes that fill out like twirling tops as the dancers spin around in one direction and jump and then reverse. Their torsos sweep in huge off-center arcs while their long, funnel-shaped sleeves brush the ground and then the sky in multiple cosmic circles. The dancers pound a mandala onto the earth with the ancient dance steps of the Black Hat masters. Occasionally, their felt boots make an audible "thwop" as the monks throw their weight into an assertive step-hop to stamp out obstacles to the dharma.

Wangchuk told me he had been in the monastery for 22 years and started learning cham when he was 11 years old. He began performing cham at the age of 19 and is now the *chamjug*, or assistant dance master, and performs the monks' entire dance repertoire. When I asked him how he prepares for his roles, he responded that he visualizes the deity he is portraying. After donning his costume, he meditates on embodying the role for the benefit of the spectators. There is no "warm-up" or physical preparation. I asked Wangchuk if he recites *mantras* (sacred syllables or phrases employed to focus the mind during meditation) while dancing. He explained that although reciting mantra is essential to performing the temple rituals that precede the cham performance, they do not recite mantras while dancing—though other monastic groups do. He disclosed that some cham require incredible stamina because of the large, heavy masks they wear during these two-to-three-hour dances. The monks dance lengthy cham during unseen preliminary temple rituals as well as in the

Text continues on page 95 ▶

FIGURE 36: (Wangchuk performing *Zhanag Cham* (Punakha Tshechu)

Zhanag Cham (BLACK HAT DANCE)

Zhanag Cham, performed today in every tshechu and many other Buddhist rituals in Bhutan (as well as in other Himalayan Buddhist areas), is a reenactment of the seminal cham ritual that is said to have been performed by Guru Rinpoche to enable the building of the first Buddhist monastery in Tibet at Samye. It is,

therefore, a prototype for cham ritual dance. To overcome the hostility to the construction project at Samye, Guru Rinpoche performed the *Vajrakilaya Cham*, in which he meditated upon and danced as the wrathful deity Vajrakīla, or Dorje Phurba in Tibetan. Vajrakīla is a yidam deity known as a fierce and powerful subduer of obstacles. In Guru Rinpoche's ritual performance, he pierced the earth with the phurba to pacify the local spirits, protect the sacred ground, prevent negative forces from reentry, and create positive conditions for the building of the monastery.

The costume, assimilated from that of pre-Buddhist magician-priests, features the recognizable round black

FIGURE 37: (Opposite) *Sachak Zhanag Cham* (Trongsa Tshechu)
FIGURE 38: (Below) *Sachak Zhanag Cham* (Trongsa Tshechu)

hat strapped to the head and a colorful, silk-brocade robe with oversize sleeves. The dancers hold a black scarf (manipulated to attract negative forces) and a ritual three-bladed dagger (symbolic of destroying obstacles, negative forces, and the ego) in the right hand and a small skull cup (representing impermanence) in the left. Over the robe they wear a long apron emblazoned with the wrathful face of a fierce deity. The design of the hat represents a mandala with the dome symbolizing Mount Meru, the figurative axis of the world. The cupola and brim are painted with magical symbols imbued with spiritual power. Various objects of symbolic meaning adorn the peak, topped by peacock feathers that signify the wish-fulfilling tree of paradise. The costume adds a palpable power to the dance-ritual.

In his book *Tibetan Religious Dances*, ethnologist René de Nebesky-Wojkowitz described the dance's origins as a magic rite enacted by lamas in order to overcome an enemy. In fact, he goes on to link its early practice to the actions of Tibetan weather-makers, who performed some form of the dance to influence the forces of nature. The dance was also employed in rites of destructive magic used for killing an enemy.[20]

The cham was famously performed by the heroic Tibetan monk Lhalungpa Pelgyi Dorji in 842 C.E. as a distraction before, in a liberating act of defending the faith, he assassinated the destructive, anti-Buddhist King Langdarma. At the climax of his cham performance he pulled a bow and arrow from his billowing sleeves and shot and slew the king. Zhabdrung Ngawang Namgyal was also legendary for his wrathful rendition of *Zhanag Cham*.[21]

The Black Hat dances are performed to pacify negative forces (literally—spirits in the earth) so that spiritual activities may proceed successfully. Performed in a number of forms (with phurba, drum, offering goblets) and involving 5–21 dancers, the dances are integral to various rituals and ceremonies important to many different occasions. The dance structure itself is used to dispense offerings and perform symbolic sacrifice and exorcism. The *Zhanag Cham* are performed at drubchen ceremonies, public empowerments, unseen temple rituals to insure the protection of the country, ground consecrations, and more.

By performing this dance, the practitioners consecrate the tshechu courtyard to become a sacred mandala—a divine palace—for the manifestation of the deities and for the spiritual transformation of the performers and viewers. *Zhanag Cham* is an example of a dance conceived and performed in pre-Buddhist times as a rite of black magic and now performed to transform the space, conditions, and community. See the cham at https://digitalcollections.nypl.org/items/d3797af0-f876-0130-e6bf-3c075448cc4b.

FIGURE 39: *Sachak Zhanag Cham* (Trongsa Tshechu)

FIGURE 40: Torma offering to the earth deities during *Sachak Zhanag Cham*

full-day public tshechu performances. Wangchuk shared this final thought: "This is not entertainment. Cham is performed for the benefit of all sentient beings to contemplate their interdependence and achieve liberation."[22]

THE CHAM TAX

The lay dancers are culled from the local communities through a type of labor tax levied on each household. Through this taxation system, ordinary people are compelled to learn the cham and folk dances in order to perform them at the festivals. I laughed when Khenpo Tashi told me this and exclaimed, "You mean there is a cham tax?" He replied, "Yes—a cham tax."

In the 1600s, Zhabdrung Ngawang Namgyal instituted a taxation system of compulsory labor for the construction of temples, dzongs, trails, and bridges, as well as contribution of food rations and supplies to support the monasteries, festivals, and government projects. Bhutan had functioned as a subsistence and barter economy until the third king, Jigme Dorji Wangchuck (r. 1952–1972), frequently called "the father of modern Bhutan," established a currency and banking system. The third king also initiated the "cham tax" so that ordinary citizens would perform the lay repertoire that had been previously performed by royal court attendants. This type of corvée had also been levied on rural families in Tibet to staff the Dalai Lama's ceremonial dance troupe and is described by Tashi Tsering in his autobiography *The Struggle for Modern Tibet*.[23] The third king introduced other cultural innovations, like the inclusion of more folk dances in the tshechu programs and the formation of RAPA, with its mandate to preserve and standardize the lay dances—both sacred and folk.

This remarkable concept of a cham tax indicates that the Bhutanese hold dance to be something of significant value. Dance is not merely a discretionary social pastime, pleasant entertainment, or fitness activity. Performing dances at a tshechu or other ritual event is of such high importance that it is considered a source of spiritual merit. Generating merit is a basic building block of Buddhist practice. In Himalayan Buddhism, one engages in virtuous acts not only to purify one's own karma (actions and their ongoing resultant effects), but *always* to extend the positive consequences to all sentient beings. If cham is considered thongdrel (capable of liberating upon sight), then just imagine the spiritual heft of performing this "tax" on behalf of one's family for the benefit of the community and even random viewers like tourists, birds, and insects.

FIGURE 41: Chimi (front row, second from the left) and women volunteer dancers perform a boedra (Punakha Tshechu).

The Mother

I spoke with a couple of the local dance volunteers to learn about their personal experiences dedicating two months to grueling rehearsals, mastering a huge body of material, and three full days of performance in service to their community and spiritual beliefs. I first visited with 20-year-old Chimi Lhaden, a young mother from the Punakha district who volunteered. Though women do not perform cham, they are active participants and performers in the folk dances. Chimi normally spends her days caring for her baby daughter and parents, as well as tending the cattle on the family farm. She found it quite overwhelming to step out of her regular sphere of activities to assume a rigorous schedule of rehearsing six days a week, eight hours per day—learning the steps, melodies, and lyrics for the 24 folk dances she performed. (Performers are expected to sing the folk songs while they are dancing.) Though Chimi wasn't sure if she would volunteer again, her beautiful face opened up as she shared how meaningful it was for her to meet and make so many new friends as this group of strangers worked together to master and perform quite complicated folk dance choreography for the tshechu.

The Farmer

Norbu Tsering, a tall, lean, 28-year-old farmer, demonstrated his innate dance and theatrical talent, performing 80 dance numbers at this tshechu. He displayed his consummate performing abilities as the Monkey in *Bardo Raksha Mangcham* (Dance of the Judgment of the Dead), the three-hour courtroom dance-drama (described in chapter 4) in which two newly deceased men are tried for their deeds to determine the realm of their next rebirth. The Monkey carries a set of scales in his hands, symbolizing how the deeds of all beings are weighed. He moves fluidly in and out of the physically challenging choreography to extemporize with the *atsaras*. These jesters, wearing big-nosed, red masks and wielding fabric or papier-mâché phalluses, cavort through the middle of the drama poking fun at the dancers with hilarious improvisations based on the actual dance steps and character roles (which they obviously know). I

was amazed at Norbu's unfazed transitions between these two polarities since, after all, he is not a trained or professional performer.

Norbu told me his favorite dance to perform is *Shawa Shachi Cham* (Dance of the Stag and the Hounds), the dance-drama, which I had seen rehearsed, about the 11th-century saint Milarepa's conversion of a hunter to Buddhism. All of the animals' choreography is organic and graceful—especially Norbu's character of the hunted stag, which is the leading role. This effectively makes the animals the sympathetic characters (as opposed to the hunter and his silly servant). The stag and two hounds hold short wooden blocks in their hands as props representing animal hooves. Accompanying the animals' dance movement is the steady, soft beating of the solo cymbal, which adds a meditative tone to the piece. The animals each perform a solo characterized by torsos describing giant arcs, followed by thrilling barrel-turn leaps. This builds to a climactic, acrobatic, double-leg extension jump, in which the hands and feet meet in the air in front of the body. Then, kneeling with their wooden hooves extended to the floor, the animals each come to rest at Milarepa's feet. The choreography always takes my breath away.

For Norbu to leave his responsibilities on the farm for two months of rehearsals could be a significant hardship for his family. When I questioned him about this, he answered that his step-father was filling in for him. When asked what the best part of the overall experience was, Norbu's ecstatic response was, "Performing all 80 dances!" He had volunteered to dance at the tshechu fully aware of the demands, as he had participated before—four years ago. Would he do it again? I got a resounding "Yes!"

Innovations

Since the time of Zhabdrung Ngawang Namgyal, the district of Punakha has celebrated an annual *drubchen*, a 21-day period of temple rituals concluding with a final day of public festival and performance. In 2005, based on requests from the people and the district administration of Punakha, the Punakha Tshechu was introduced by the 70th Je Khenpo, Trulku Jigme Choedra, and the Home Minister, His Excellency Lyonpo Jigme Yoedzer Thinley. In honor of the Punakha Tshechu, which follows on the heels of the Punakha Drubchen, Dasho Ramjam Thinley Gyamtsho, then principal of RAPA, was commissioned to choreograph a dance work to inaugurate the event. The result was the *Zhabdrung Zednam* (The Coming of the Zhabdrung) a three-day spectacle, recounting the history of Zhabdrung Ngawang Namgyal. The local crowd seemed attentive and thrilled with the grand display.

Text continues on page 102 ▶

Zhabdrung Zednam (The Coming of the Zhabdrung)

Zhabdrung Zednam was choreographed by Thinley Gyamtsho, former principal of RAPA, to inaugurate the Punakha Tshechu in 2005. Using newly constructed sets and creative props and costumes, the *Zednam* incorporates specific regional folk dances as they might have been performed during the historic events from the Zhabdrung's life dramatized in the production. For example, the *Goen Zhey* is performed in a scene portraying the people of the Gasa district as they welcome the Zhabdrung upon his escape from Tibet. There is a creative tableau depicting the building of the great Punakha Dzong. Battle scenes between the Bhutanese and Tibetans are feisty and sometimes incorporate cham movements, which is fitting since cham often

involves wrathful energy as well as victorious themes. Sections of the *Zednam* are interspersed with the usual performances of cham and folk dance over the three-day tshechu program. The spectacle concludes with a great religious procession, featuring a monk dressed in robes and a mask as the Zhabdrung, followed by a dedication ceremony overflowing with devotional folk dances. This is how the Bhutanese honor important religious masters to this day.

FIGURE 43: (Opposite) *Zhabdrung Zednam—Goen Zhey* (Punakha Tshechu)

FIGURE 44: (Below) *Zhabdrung Zednam—Battle against Tibetans* (Punakha Tshechu)

I met Dasho Thinley Gyamtsho afterward. He told me with a sense of excitement, "It is still a work in progress." With new segments added this year, he has plans to make further additions next year.

Part of RAPA's mission is to give support and training to local communities to preserve their intangible culture. In preparation for the Punakha Tshechu, RAPA assigned two cham dancers and one female folk dancer to train the local volunteers for two months. In addition, four RAPA musicians joined the final two weeks of rehearsals and then performed live at the tshechu.

Looking to the Future through the Past

Khenpo Tashi worries that traditional Bhutanese culture may disappear in 20 years due to the intrusion of Western culture and values. I would guess that he, as the director of the country's national museum, has his finger on the pulse of the people and their involvement with the culture. But I think his prediction may be too pessimistic. Bhutan's culture has shown a high degree of resilience through the ages—often as the result of decisions made by wise leaders who understood the importance of a thriving culture to the identity of the nation and the unity of its people. The Bhutanese culture benefitted from the "treasure tradition" that offered a system for reformulating practices and expressions (including cham) of foundational religious concepts. In the 1600s, the code of cultural etiquette and institution of sacred festivals formalized under the leadership of the Zhabdrung and his successors defined and distinguished a national Bhutanese culture. In the 1900s, through his tax compelling citizens to perform in their local festivals and by creating RAPA to preserve and protect Bhutan's sacred and traditional performing arts, the third king promoted cultural knowledge and community vitality. The fourth king of Bhutan, Jigme Singye Wangchuck (r. 1972–2006), introduced the economic/development policy called Gross National Happiness, which includes the key guideline to preserve and promote the country's unique traditional culture. In the last few years, the government has created new local festivals with historical and environmental themes, commissioning new works to celebrate them. Bhutan has consistently innovated in the service of promoting and honoring its cultural heritage.

There are, however, cultural and religious institutions in other countries that have taken interventions to extend their significance and longevity by inviting women into ritual performances that were previously only for men. A couple of nunneries in India and Nepal already encourage the nuns to perform cham and female lay members perform sacred dances in some Buddhist communities in the West. Bhutan has yet to do that. I can imagine initiating this innovation with the *dakini* dances. After all, the *Dances of the Sixteen Dakinis*, performed as part of the grand homage to Guru Rinpoche within *Guru Tshengye Cham*, are a presentation of gifts to the Guru from these emanations of feminine energy. Involving monastic women in the performance of the dakini cham as the important facilitators in tantric Buddhist practice that they have historically been might be a good place to take that next evolutionary step.

FIGURE 45: Monks dancing (Trongsa)

Since returning from Bhutan, I have been reading Khenpo Tashi's recent book, *Three Rising Stars: Amazing Life Stories of the Enlightened Masters of Bhutan*, the sacred biographies of his three religious teachers, or masters. As I read about the travels and activities that fill the lives of Bhutan's monks and lamas—empowerments, dedications, drubchen, longevity prayers, temple consecrations, and numerous rituals—I realize something profound from my discussions with the khenpo. Though the words on the pages of text don't specifically say so (because the Bhutanese inherently know this), all of these events and rituals involve performing cham. The monks and lamas were dancing—all the time.

PART IV:
East Meets West in Texas

CHAPTER EIGHT

Opera Bhutan—Transcending Borders

EARLY IN 2013, I received an email from Tshering, the vice principal of RAPA, describing a most unlikely project—a cross-cultural collaboration called "Opera Bhutan." The project was the brainchild of baroque music specialist and conductor, Aaron Carpenè, who had the novel idea to produce the first Western opera in Bhutan. It would be a collaboration uniting elements of Bhutan's performing arts traditions with the Western operatic form. The chosen opera, *Acis and Galatea* by George Frederic Handel, with its story based on a Greek myth retold in Ovid's *Metamorphoses*, seemed the perfect platform. It shares many universal themes that resonate in Buddhism—love, suffering as a result of anger and attachment, and death leading to transformation.

Even more curious than the production itself, was that it was being sponsored by the University of Texas at El Paso (UTEP) and would eventually be performed there, in the west Texas border town better known for college basketball and sometimes prickly border tensions with its Mexican neighbor Ciudad Juarez. I wasn't entirely surprised about the sponsorship of the production; I was familiar with the Bhutan-UTEP connection.

BACKGROUND

The curious link between UTEP and Bhutan began one hundred years ago when the wife of the first dean of the school, Kathleen Worrell, read a 1914 *National Geographic* article. The photo essay described the travels of Jean Claude White, a colonial officer stationed in the Raj (British Empire in India), who trekked across the isolated mountain kingdom of Bhutan. From

White's early photos of the Himalayas, she imagined a resemblance to El Paso's Franklin Mountains and convinced her husband that Bhutan's architecture would be a good model for the university buildings that needed reconstructing after a fire. Since then, UTEP's buildings conform to the unique style of Bhutan—battered walls tapering outward at the base, a wide reddish band painted around the upper portion of the facade, Bhutanese designs dotting the band and the painted borders around the windows, and red roofs crowned by golden pinnacles. Over the years the relationship between UTEP and Bhu-

FIGURE 46: UTEP campus architecture (El Paso, Texas)

tan has been nurtured to include frequent cultural events, student exchange, and—Opera Bhutan.

When UTEP president Dr. Diana Natalicio first encountered the campus architecture, she appreciated its serenity and tranquility. During her 30-year tenure at UTEP, she has sought to strengthen the university's relationship with the Himalayan nation—beyond the buildings. The school has encouraged a steady presence of Bhutanese exchange students. UTEP has a history of programming "Bhutan Days," during which they display and demonstrate examples of the culture that coincide with the architecture they inhabit. Since archery is the much loved national sport of Bhutan, the university held an archery demonstration in their Sun Bowl football stadium. As the Bhutanese are ace archers, well practiced at shooting at targets placed 140 meters away, the very first arrow was shot with such force that it flew out of the stadium and into the parking lot. Luckily no one was felled.

The new centerpiece of the campus is an authentic Bhutanese *lhakhang* (Buddhist temple). It had been designed in Bhutan as part of an exhibition for the 2008 Smithsonian Folklife Festival in Washington, D. C. After the culmination of the festival, the lhakhang was given to the school. Disassembled, transported, stored, and now reconstructed, the lhakhang was painstakingly refurbished by Bhutanese artisans in preparation for its early 2015 opening as a campus intercultural center.

The Idea

Back in 2004, Aaron Carpenè took his Opera Bhutan concept to Preston Scott, consultant to the Bhutanese government and curator for the Smithsonian Folklife Festival: Bhutan exhibition. In 2009 they proposed the idea to Bhutanese officials. Once the Bhutanese government expressed interest in hosting its first opera production, Carpenè approached Italian stage director, Stefano Vizioli, who was enticed by the novelty of the project and its potential for learning and reaching beyond the ordinary. Next, they would have to find a sponsoring partner.

After several rejections from various opera companies, Scott reached out to

Dr. Natalicio and UTEP. In 2012, seeking new ways to strengthen the university's relationship with Bhutan and because of her own vision for her students and the larger El Paso community, Dr. Natalicio threw her support behind Opera Bhutan and its creators. The plan was to premiere the opera in Bhutan in October 2013 and, a year later, in Texas for UTEP's centennial.

Teaching at a school with a population of 23,000 students, whose demographics reflect those of the region—78 percent Mexican American and another 8 percent who commute across the border from Juarez—Dr. Natalicio is committed to creating the highest quality educational opportunities for a historically underserved population. Through Opera Bhutan, UTEP students, performing in the opera chorus and orchestra (along with some faculty), would work professionally with international vocalists and opera directors, travel and work abroad in a completely foreign culture when the production premiered in Bhutan, and create an invaluable experience for their own community on the occasion of the university's centennial celebration. Dr. Natalicio, a picture of sage elegance—with measured words, a knowing smile, and her pure white hair swept up in a bun—acknowledged, "Creating a dissonance by producing a baroque/Bhutanese fusion opera on the Texas/Mexico border will cause people to scratch their heads and be curious to learn more about us."[24]

The directors wanted to achieve an authentic expression that would honor each culture's interpretation of the dramatic material. To that end, the main production team traveled to Bhutan to meet and begin the collaboration with the artists at RAPA.

My Invitation

Tshering recounted how Vizioli described the story of *Acis and Galatea* and blocked the opera into scenes. Together they decided where to incorporate elements of the country's sacred dance, folk music, and folk dance. Tshering made selections from their repertoire that enriched the telling of the story from the Bhutanese perspective. Periodically logging onto the Opera Bhutan website and watching posted video clips of their rehearsals on the outdoor court at RAPA headquarters, I followed their progress on the project.

Tshering had invited me to attend the production in El Paso. The idea that I might be able to see friends and dances from Bhutan amidst Bhutanese architecture without flying all the way to Bhutan was an inviting thought. I am also a native Texan and could combine a trip to El Paso with a visit to my family. I would go!

I could see the brownish-pink desert plains of west Texas from the airplane window as we approached. From the airport, we sped by the nearby mountains in Juarez where the graffiti scratched into the rock face exhorts, "*Lee la Biblia. Es la verdad.*" (Read the Bible. It is the truth.) Then I arrived at the university where, strangely, under the blazing desert sun, the buildings cohere to the fortress style and design of the remote Himalayan nation of Bhutan, albeit with a pinkish tinge. They had even erected stately, vertical, multicolored prayer flags to scatter Buddhist prayers across the campus grounds. Shangri-la had come to Texas!

As I walked to the venue to attend a dress rehearsal, my jaw dropped as I realized we were entering the university's huge Don Haskins Center, a basketball arena that seats 12,000 people. I am not used to that level of opera attendance—even in my hometown of New York City. Dr. Natalicio smiled as she told me they hoped for at least 7500 to attend the free event, "a gift the school is presenting to the community in celebration of our centennial."

Backstage, in the RAPA dressing room, usually quarters for UTEP's famed basketball players, I couldn't help but notice the cultural dissonance between the UTEP star players' posters plastered on the walls and the sacred dance masks and instruments of the Bhutanese dancers. The dancers donned layer after layer of costume infused with Himalayan Buddhist symbolism—colorful silk skirts, shirts, collars, belts, sashes, wigs, and crowns—fully transforming themselves into performers of a sacred tradition.

The Performance

On the evening of the centennial performance, the arena began to fill with students, faculty, families from El Paso and from Juarez, friends (some of whom worked on the production in Bhutan), and alumni of all ages. The RAPA

dancers opened the evening with two sacred dances from the cham repertoire, *Pacham* (Dance of the Heroes) and *Dramitse Nga Cham* (The Drum Dance of Dramitse). This pre-performance treat gave the audience a glimpse into the powerful, danced Buddhist practice of cham.

Vizioli envisioned staging the production in a manner that would capture the atmosphere of a Bhutanese *tshechu*. In these outdoor courtyard performances the audience is arranged around the performance space at the same level as and in close proximity to the performers. Hence, the stage for the opera at UTEP was built jutting out into the audience. Sometimes the main characters, chorus, and Bhutanese dancers made their entrances at audience level (below the stage) and proceeded around the stage before climbing up or even leaping onto it.

Acis and Galatea, a baroque pastoral opera, originally premiered in 1718 as a courtly entertainment for a private gathering in the English countryside. Sung in English (which is Bhutan's second language), the opera's simple plot is a tragic love triangle. Acis, a young shepherd, falls in love with the sea-nymph Galatea. Unfortunately, the cyclops (monster) Polyphemus has also been smitten by Galatea's beauty. Unable to control his jealousy, Polyphemus hurls a huge stone at Acis and kills him. The chorus consoles Galatea, convincing her to use her semidivine powers to transform her dead lover into a flowing stream, immortalizing him.

To more effectively integrate the Bhutanese cultural elements into the Handel opera, Vizioli reimagined the story. He set it in the early 1920s with a group of young European travelers, following in the footsteps of Jean Claude White, as they visit Bhutan for the first time. Galatea, sung with playful virtuosity, was portrayed as a member of the group of Western tourists. Carrying a copy of the historic issue of *National Geographic* from April 1914, as if using the photo essay as her guidebook to the surrounding foreign sights, she made her initial entrance through the yellow silk curtains (reminiscent of Bhutanese temple and tshechu decor).

The chorus, Galatea's Western traveling companions, dressed in 1920s period attire, performed pleasing choreography that integrated steps and formations from English country dances.

FIGURE 47: (Opposite) A RAPA dancer backstage donning the five-lobed crown to dance *Pacham* (El Paso, Texas)

The Bhutanese performers supported the action as the Western travelers played out their drama. The female Bhutanese vocalist sang a newly composed song with a haunting melody called "The Four Friends," based on a Buddhist teaching about the interconnectedness of all beings. She was accompanied by four Bhutanese masked dancers wearing typical cham costumes—multicolored silk skirts, silk tops, and animal masks—and dancing an ersatz sacred dance. The presentation captured characteristic sights and sounds of Bhutan.

At times the masked dancers moved about the main players in a slow surreal fashion. With their mythical presence, they served as a kinetic stage set, facilitating the characters' progress through the plot.

A contemporary Bhutanese love song, with an accompanying folk dance, was woven into the story. The movements were gentle and flowing, with fluid hand and wrist gestures—always made to look effortless in typical Bhutanese style. The dancers were dressed in their traditional attire (different from the sacred dance costumes): the men wore red and gold-striped *gho* and special embroidered knee-high boots, and the vocalist wore a salmon-colored brocade *kira* topped off with an elegant matching silk *toego* (women's jacket). The folk dance and song had a magical quality as the folk dancers encircled Acis and Galatea, who were seated on the floor performing a mirroring sequence that communicated their enrapt state.

No sooner than we were carried away with the soaring emotions and music of the young lovers, the winds of change and turbulence danced through in the form of Bhutanese masked performers. Wearing wrathful, red masks and tiger-skin skirts, they danced bare-chested, using hooked sticks to loudly beat large hand drums. The choreography incorporated movements from sacred dances that depict spirits who subjugate obstacles and negativity. Their bounding onto the stage to form a circle of pounding drums and frightening costumes set an alarming and sinister tone—foreshadowing impending doom for the idyllic love affair.

On opposite sides of the stage, two silk-skirted Bhutanese dancers blowing the dramatic ten-foot-long dungchen heralded the entrance of the giant monster Polyphemus. He, with his rich bass voice, sang of his intense attraction to Galatea, when all of a sudden two *atsaras* (Bhutanese jesters) sauntered onto the stage. These jokers, costumed in red pajamas and red masks with a fabric phallus flopping around on top, were cleverly integrated as confidants to whom Polyphemus bemoaned his lack of romantic success. Inspecting Polyphemus's manhood and sniffing up his cloak and body parts to assess his physical fitness, the atsaras used all their irreverent antics to make fun of his pathetic attempts to woo Galatea.

The opera hit a moving climax as Acis and Galatea sang a public declaration of their love. The sublime strains were joined by a jealous Polyphemus, who transformed it into an emotion-filled trio, until he could no longer contain his rage and killed Acis, crushing him with a boulder.

Figure 48: Scene from Opera Bhutan (El Paso, Texas) Photo credit: J.R. Hernandez / UTEP News Service

In a well-crafted and poignant transition, a solitary, barefoot Bhutanese flute player performing a traditional tune walked onstage as Acis lay dead. As he finished, four masked dancers in the white skeleton costumes of the *Durdag Cham* (Lords of the Cremation Grounds Dance) performed sections of this sacred dance around Acis's dead body. They shook the fingers of their floppy white gloves and twisted their bodies back and forth. These lords are believed to dwell in the cremation grounds to help liberate those who have departed.

A solo Bhutanese vocalist, dressed as an enlightened lama, accompanied the dancers and sang as he circumambulated the stage. He chanted a mournful melody with lyrics, composed by the revered 11th-century yogi Milarepa, which spoke, once again, of the interconnectedness of all beings.

After a moving choral procession and lament, the chorus convinced Galatea to immortalize Acis by transforming him into a flowing stream. The Bhutanese performers facilitated this final act in an exquisitely staged metamorphosis. They carried a giant, blue, silk cloth and placed it over Acis. Galatea, emerging from her grief, wrapped herself in the blue silk as if it were an all-encompassing cloak. The Bhutanese performed a folk dance encircling her; the chorus unfurled the remainder of the blue cloth to cover the entire stage and gently manipulated it to create the vision of a rippling stream. As Galatea released the cloak, she turned upstage and walked amidst the ripples, having transformed her lover and having been transformed by loving. The finale was breathtaking.

Observations and Insights

Opera Bhutan's syncretic interpretation was affecting on so many levels. The process employed to create the piece entailed thought, dialogue, cooperation, and compromise—skills we sorely need in the domains of domestic, national, and global relations. Artists from distinct cultures learned and contributed their unique expressions of shared themes and values—amplifying the range of expressivity.

The opportunities for the varied audiences to gain exposure to new sights, sounds, and expressions raised the potential for resonating connections. Both

East and West sacrificed some cultural purity for the sake of the production, but the collaborative process itself was an authentic artistic expression.

The Opera Bhutan directors are creating more waves in the opera world and have received proposals for more intercultural collaborative projects. In Japan during October of 2016, they produced *JapanOrfeo*, fusing the Monteverdi opera with performances by masters of the Hosho School of Noh Theatre and the Fujima School of Nihon Buyo (traditional Japanese dance) and they workshopped *The Magic Flute* in Cambodia, with performances in early 2018. Carpenè and Vizioli have an infectious enthusiasm. When Carpenè expounds upon any piece of baroque opera, there is nothing more exciting in the world. Vizioli then brings it into a brilliant visual reality with his big, warm, demonstrative, Italian heart. They are quite a duo!

The UTEP student performers and their families, some of whom cross the border every time they travel to and from the university, described in their blogposts from Bhutan how they were utterly changed by participating in a creative process drawing on artistic and cultural expressions that transcend political boundaries and geographic borders. The university offered an unprecedented opportunity for exposure and learning to its students, the surrounding communities, and the Bhutanese collaborating artists and audiences.

Remarkably, the Western classical myth of Acis and Galatea served as a perfect vehicle to illustrate the Himalayan Buddhist view of the transitory nature of the physical world. Opera Bhutan then took this tale of transformation through love and added its own unique story of reaching across cultures—achieving an expression that transcends the ordinary and builds bridges instead of walls. Shangri-la is truly a state of mind rather than a place. And yes, with Opera Bhutan, a border town in Texas was transformed into Shangri-la.

Part V:
Searching for Treasure

CHAPTER NINE

The Sacred Valley and the Treasure

My fourth trip to Bhutan took me to Bumthang in search of a treasure. This central region of the country, comprised of four valleys, has long been considered the spiritual center of Bhutan. Bumthang was the site of many of the country's sacred myths, miracles, and historical events and has been the seat of many of Bhutan's most revered lamas. Bumthang is also believed to be the first locale in Bhutan to be visited in the mid-eighth century by Guru Rinpoche, the all-powerful tantric mystic from India who is credited with paving the way for the flourishing of Buddhism in Tibet and Bhutan, and who is worshipped across the country as the Second Buddha.

There are numerous oral variations on this story, but most Bhutanese seem to agree on this much: A king from northern India, named Sindhu Raja, established himself as the King of Bumthang. He got into a scrape with rival Indian King Nawoche, resulting in the death of Sindhu Raja's only son. The king was so distraught over the circumstances that he subsequently offended the chief Bumthang deity, Shelging Karpo. The deity took revenge by turning the skies black and stealing King Sindhu Raja's life force. One of the king's men implored the Vajrayana master, Guru Rinpoche, to come to Bumthang to save Sindhu Raja.

The Guru arrived in Bumthang and requested a consort with whom he could carry out the mystical practices that would cure the king. Sindhu Raja assigned his most virtuous daughter, Tashi Kheudren, to this task and she and the Guru retreated to a cave for meditative practice. The oral accounts become quite dramatic at this point and suggest that Guru Rinpoche transformed into his eight manifestations (he circulated throughout the region taking on various wrathful and peaceful aspects to heroically "save the day") and together he and his consort danced a powerful tantric cham.

Finding the spectacle irresistible, the stubborn Shelging Karpo ventured out—but in the form of a snow lion. The Guru immediately transformed into a *garuda* (mythical bird creature), alighted, and seized the snow lion extracting his vow to behave and become a loyal protector of Buddhism. Thus, having saved Sindhu Raja's life, Guru Rinpoche went on to make peace between the two kings and sealed the agreement at a stone pillar at Nabji. He converted them both to Buddhism and instructed them in its ways.

This narrative provides a glimpse of the transformative power attributed to dance in Bhutanese myth and ritual as well as the importance of Bumthang in connecting the country with its most important spiritual figure.

The Treasure

The treasure for which I came searching was dance—for much of Himalayan Buddhist revelation came in the form of dance. Unlike some other religious traditions, Himalayan Buddhism does not renounce the physical body, but rather utilizes it as one of three doors—body, speech, and mind—through which spiritual wisdom, action, and transformation are expressed. Through Vajrayana techniques of body, speech, and mind, the practitioner works to transform himself or herself into the body, speech, and mind of a buddha.

Cham and the performance of mudras, or gestures, are sacred arts of the body. They are used to full effect—with accompanying ritual music, dramatic masks, and elaborately adorned costumes rich in symbolic iconography—to ignite the senses with spiritual messages. In Himalayan Buddhism, the cham are an essential element of ritual and ceremony used to express all that is sacred—welcoming, offering, appeasement, subjugation, liberation, power, victory, compassion, and more. Inner meditation is combined with outer physical performance in a ritual process, integrating mind and body—both required for transformation to take place.

The dance treasure for which I came searching is a repertoire of dances called tercham. These dances are believed to be *terma*, which are treasures hidden by Guru Rinpoche and his immediate disciples for discovery by future generations during times of spiritual need. Some treasure dances were derived from terma discovered as texts, while others were received as revelation during dream or meditative states by many of the famous spiritual masters called *terton*, or treasure revealers, some of whom practiced and taught in the Bumthang Valley. Some of these dances were written down and others were simply orally preserved.

The treasure tradition was institutionalized and so richly developed by the *Nyingmapa* (followers of the oldest school of Himalayan Buddhism) that there are several categories of treasure revelation. Some of the dances are considered *dagnang* (pure vision) and others are *gongter*, or "mind-to-mind" treasure, in that they were revealed directly into the mindstream of the discoverer. The terton are generally held to be reincarnations of Guru Rinpoche's 25 original disciples. It follows that the wisdom and practices they rediscover are the wisdom and practices originally taught by Guru Rinpoche.

Terton Dorje Lingpa

The great terton whose footsteps and choreography I was following through the Bhutanese treasure ground was Terton Dorje Lingpa (1346–1405). He is considered to be one of the five great treasure revealers among the Nyingmapa. Dorje Lingpa was born in central Tibet and given the name Orgyen Zangpo. He travelled about Tibet and Bhutan revealing hidden manuscripts and visions that described a radical approach to spiritual practice in that it acknowledged treasures from both Buddhism and *Bon* (the pre-Buddhist, indigenous religious tradition of the region). By the age of 17, he became known as Dorje Lingpa. (Lingpa is a title used to designate a terton, or treasure revealer.) At times, when revealing Bon treasure texts, he used the name Bonzhig Lingpa. Along with his envisioned treasure dances, Dorje Lingpa is also credited with disclosing numerous caches, across the landscape of Tibet and Bhutan, containing doctrinal treasures, sacred images, and sacramental objects as well as instructions for hundreds of rites for empowerment, consecration, taking vows, repentance, burnt offerings, and subjugation.

FIGURE 49: Terton Dorje
Lingpa—the central figure
from a thangka at Buli
Monastery (permission to
photograph and publish
granted by Buli Monastery)

Jampa Lhakhang Drub Overview

I was visiting Bumthang at the end of October to attend the Jampa Lhakhang Drub, an annual community festival and one of a handful of places where the treasure dances of Dorje Lingpa are performed.

I have already explained that Vajrayana Buddhism is an amalgamation of pre-Buddhist indigenous practices as well as tenets and practices of Buddhism introduced from India. The Jampa Lhakhang festival very clearly bears traces of pre-Buddhist folk rites—a naked dance, fire rituals, a fertility rite, and an exorcism—but they occur in a Buddhist context with a Buddhist message.

A major point of departure for Buddhism from the earlier folk traditions was the strong disavowal of animal sacrifice to numerous local deities. Symbolic sacrifice, overlaid with a distinctly Buddhist message, however, is quite pervasive in Vajrayana practice. Tantric gurus, yogis, *siddhas* (mystics), and dakinis devised countless methods for overcoming life's obstacles and enemies—both external and internal. Whether the obstacle was the entrenched power structure and its resistance to a new Buddhist belief system; obstacles inherent in the struggle for human survival such as sickness, starvation, disaster, warfare, or wild animals; or the challenges of one's own inner demons and ego, the terton and the lamas employed skillful means (ritual, meditation, complex visualizations, mantra, dance) for dealing with it. That is essentially what this annual *drub* (consecration), with its many detailed rituals and cham, is—a community effort to meet the challenges of life and uplift itself for the coming year.

CHAPTER TEN

Meeting the Chakar Lama

Aboard the 48-seat DrukAir prop plane on a pristine day, I made the storybook domestic flight with eyepopping views of the major snowy peaks of the eastern Himalayas—Chomolhari, Jichu Drake, Table Mountain (Kanchen Singye), and Gangar Pensum—into Bumthang. All of these peaks are off-limits to technical mountain climbers out of deference to the mountain deities who abide there. Twenty-five minutes later I landed on a runway in the middle of golden buckwheat fields next to a one-room airport that doesn't even claim a security scanning machine.

Bumthang is comprised of four valleys—Chume, Chokhor, Tang, and Ura. I was heading to the Chokhor (Iron) Valley to visit Chakar Lam Dorje, the then 88-year-old lineage holder—keeper and guardian of Dorje Lingpa's dance and ritual traditions. I stopped at a general store in the center of town to purchase a white silk khata to offer to him. Once again, I rehearsed this gestural expression of respect and gratitude with my guide, as I had grown a little rusty since my last khata presentation. Although the Lama (Chakar Lam Dorje) had just been discharged from the hospital, he agreed to meet with me, and we drove off toward his house. Our driver stopped along the roadside to give a lift to a little old man with a cane out for a mid-morning walk. He chatted in Dzongkha with my guide and driver. As we pulled into the driveway of the Lama's house, my guide said to me, "You can give the Lama the khata when you get out of the car." I thought to myself, "Well, of course I can. That was the plan." The driver leaned over and whispered the same instructions to me. It was then it dawned on me that our backseat passenger *was* the Lama.

THE CHAKAR LAMA

The Lama's house and the Chakar *Lhakhang* (temple) next door are said to be built on the site of King Sindhu Raja's nine-story iron palace. Chakar Lam Dorje explained that the palace was destroyed by the anti-Buddhist King

Langdarma (803–842) and Dorje Lingpa restored the temple and its relics. According to Tibetan and Bon scholar Dr. Samten Karmay, Dorje Lingpa spent just under three years in Bumthang (1374–1376) and is supposed to have lived in the residence occupied by Chakar Lam Dorje today.[25]

My guide and I, along with our driver who is a local hotelier in the Chokhor valley, went into the Lama's house and upstairs to his sitting room where we were offered tea and cookies. The Chakar Lama is a non-monastic, married, lay priest called a *gomchen*, which means "great meditator." In Bhutan, where the aspiration of "attaining enlightenment" is not uncommon, there are many different types of religious practitioners. There are celibate monastics (nuns and monks) and then there are either married or celibate reincarnate lamas, hereditary lamas, lamas who simply undertake the studies to become spiritual teachers and practitioners, and lay practitioners. The Lama is a practitioner of the Nyingma tradition as was Dorje Lingpa. The Nyingma School maintains a direct, experiential connection with Padmasambhava, which helps explain what the treasure tradition is really all about—a continuous rediscovery and reiteration of Guru Rinpoche's teachings and practices. As the Lama had been apprised of my interest in Dorje Lingpa's tercham tradition, we launched into the interview in Dzongkha with my guide and driver serving as translators.

The drub takes place just down the road from the Chakar Lama's residence at Jampa Lhakhang, which is dedicated to the Buddha of the Future—*Jampa* (Tibetan) or *Maitreya* (Sanskrit). Dating from the mid-seventh century, it is one of the oldest temples in Bhutan. Like Kyichu Lhakhang in Paro, it is attributed to King Songtsen Gampo and is one of the fabled 108 temples built in a single day to restrain the giant ogress believed to have been obstructing the establishment of Buddhism in the region. Jampa Lhakhang was situated to pin down her left knee. The temple fell into disrepair, and Dorje Lingpa commenced its restoration around 1388. His spiritual son (reincarnation) Trulku Chokten Gonpo is responsible for building the giant, gold, seated statue of Jampa—the centerpiece of the temple. It is he who appointed the first Chakar Lama as caretaker of the temple, and the Chakar Lama's descendants have maintained the temple and Dorje Lingpa's traditions ever since.

Conversation about the Jampa Lhakhang Drub

Chakar Lam Dorje's earliest childhood memories of the Jampa Lhakhang Drub are of how his parents worked exceedingly hard to produce the event. At the age of 12 he started learning the cham. His father passed away quite young, so his uncle taught him the dances. By the age of 20 he had become the *champon* (dance master), shouldering the responsibility for maintaining the treasure dances of Dorje Lingpa. Dorje Lingpa's dances and ritual cycles are performed at only a few places in Bhutan—the nearby Buli Monastery, Dangchu Goemba (Sephu), Drangla (Trongsa), Nabji Temple, and Ogyen Choling Estate (prayers and rituals only/no cham). After restoring Jampa Lhakhang, Dorje Lingpa initiated the festival and envisioned the dances. The word "*drub*" is not usually used for "festival," which is generally called a tshechu. *Drub* means "consecration," so the Jampa Lhakhang Drub is an annual reconsecration of the temple. Chakar Lam Dorje feels his primary responsibility as the Chakar Lama is to organize the drub every year. Nowadays, the Lama's eldest son Tenzin, having performed as the champon for many years, has taken on these responsibilities as well as the job of training the community's cham dancers.

According to Chakar Lam Dorje, the overall structure of the drub was conceived by Dorje Lingpa. Initially, the Fire Offering and ensuing cham on the first night establish the sacred space. The drub proceeds in three parts: *Tsukton* (Beginning), *Barton* (Middle), and *Jugton* (Conclusion). The Tsukton marks the beginning of the festival proper and the program consists of many typical cham. The Barton features more cham, and culminates inside the temple with several prayer cycles (all of which are Dorje Lingpa terma) followed by a ritual called *torgyab* (a symbolic exorcism), performed for the benefit of the community. On the final day, the Jugton dispenses good feelings with celebratory spirit as the crowd lines up to enter the temple and receive blessings from the treasure relics kept inside. Simultaneously, outside, the dancers perform the unique treasure dances of Dorje Lingpa. When I asked what was the most important moment of the drub, the Chakar Lama replied, "The fire offering ceremony." He continued, "It is important because we are ridding the community and, by extension, the entire country and, by extension, the whole universe of all obstacles and negativity for the coming year. It is a big responsibility on behalf of so many."

The Chakar Lama maintains that he pretty much sticks to the festival program that has been set for centuries and makes only occasional changes. The drub preparations begin one month in advance with cham rehearsals. As confirmed by his son and another community leader, in an old tradition, each year, every household must contribute three people (two dancers and one cook/server) to produce the drub, which is the combined effort of three villages. I was familiar with this compulsory "cham tax" from my previous discussions with Khenpo Tashi. The Lama reported that his first preparation is setting up the offerings inside the temple. This festival, like other festivals in Bhutan, is preceded by a ten-day *drubchen* (purification ceremony of prayers and rituals performed by monks inside the temple).

When I asked about the biggest challenge to maintaining the drub, the Lama, with a grounded sense of practicality, responded, "Funding!" There is no government support, as it is considered a small community festival. As a result, they cannot provide financial incentives for the dancers, most of whom have family and farming responsibilities and sometimes don't show up to rehearsals. They also experience difficulty in getting the elaborate costumes sewn. This grand event does, however, have some private funding from the tourist industry, which is a sound investment, given that the festival, aside from its spiritual importance to the local participants, is a popular draw for tourists and therefore a boon to the industry and local economy.

The Chakar Lama's Temple

Following our three-hour conversation, the Lama agreed to take me next door and show me the Chakar Temple. We climbed the stairs up to the padlocked temple door, which he opened. After removing our shoes, we mounted a steep, wooden, ladder-like stairway and walked through a curtain-draped doorway into the temple proper, filled with treasures that would be featured during the festival ahead. The altar was set with typical offerings—brass and silver bowls of water, platters of fruit, multicolored torma, and two brass ewers of holy water, each ewer topped with a peacock feather. At each end of the altar was a column on which hung the buffalo masks of the wrathful Lord of Death (Shinje) and his consort. They would be worn for *Shinje Yab-Yum*, one of the festival's opening cham.

Behind the altar, in glass-enclosed cabinets, were the usual icons—statues of Guru Rinpoche, his main consorts, the Buddha, Zhabdrung Ngawang Namgyal, deities, and bodhisattvas. The cabinets also displayed a collection of local treasures, including a golden statue of Tashi Kheudren—famed daughter of the Bumthang King Sindhu Raja—who became the Bhutanese consort of Guru Rinpoche (partnering with him to perform many of his amazing miracles). She was dressed in a striped, silk kira and draped in jewelry. Nearby was a footprint believed to be hers. Another cabinet contained a golden statue of Dorje Lingpa holding a damaru in his right hand. He was flanked on the left by a figure of the first Chakar Lama and on the right by a figure of Dorje Lingpa's spiritual son. In a few days these singular items and other relevant relics—like a *phurbu* (small ritual dagger), dorje, and knotted sword—would be paraded in a procession, indicating the start of the festival, from the Chakar Lhakhang to the Jampa Lhakhang.

To the right of the glass cabinets were shelves stacked with cloth-wrapped tablets of Dorje Lingpa terma discovered in scriptural form. Covering the left wall of the temple was a large, brightly colored *thangka* (religious painting on silk) of Dorje Lingpa. He wears flowing orange robes and holds a damaru in his right hand and a ritual bell in his left, clearly engaged in Buddhist ritual practice. He sits before a low altar table with various ritual objects and is encircled by an aura of rainbow light. Dorje Lingpa is surrounded by pink lotuses and peonies with interwoven greenery. Above the central figure sits a row of tantric deities in meditative postures. Scholarly lamas of the lineage surround the terton along the sides and across the bottom. After we had time to admire the beautiful work of art, the Chakar Lama closed the yellow silk curtains that protect the painting's brilliant colors from the sun light streaming in through the adjacent window.

We continued downstairs to the mask room filled with inanimate, wrathful, and comedic cham masks hanging on long iron nails waiting for action. Drums, swords, and animal masks lay strewn about on one table and peacock feather–topped, tantric, black hats rested on another—all silently auguring the magic steps to come.

FIGURE 52: Thangka of Dorje Lingpa inside the Chakar Lhakhang (permission to photograph and publish granted by Chakar Lam Dorje)

Figure 53: Cham masks hanging in the Chakar Lhakhang mask room

CHAPTER ELEVEN

Double Sighting (The Consecration)

A WONDERFUL SURPRISE awaited me the next morning! I learned that there would be a once-in-a-lifetime *thongdrel* consecration at Jampa Lhakhang before the onset of the drub the next day. The November early morning air was crisp and the sky was clear as we hurried along the village road packed with cars, pedestrians, and the occasional cow.

The massive 50-by-40-foot, appliqué, silk tapestry in brilliant jewel tones features a huge image of Buddha Maitreya seated upright, Western-style—as he is frequently depicted—ready to arise in response to the needs of the world and serve as the Buddha of the Future. He is surrounded above by an inner circle of buddhas and bodhisattvas and, at the level of his lotus throne, by dancing wrathful deities. Lineage holders form an outer constellation. Below the giant figure of Maitreya sit two royal kings—Sindhu Raja of Bumthang to the left and Trisong Deutsen of Tibet to the right. Intermingled are several wrathful deities emitting bright flames from their dancing bodies. The spectacular work of religious art was unfurled from tall poles on the temple grounds. Usually these tapestries are displayed once a year during the early hours of the final day of a tshechu. Then they are carefully lowered, folded, carried in a coordinated procession, and stored in a long, casket-like box before the sun's rays can damage the rich colors and fine fabric. If you are really lucky, you might even see a couple of sacred dances performed before such a dazzling backdrop.

A thongdrel is a type of mandala, a sacred diagram or space, used to promote spiritual process. It is considered such a potent symbol and meditation aid that it has the power to liberate merely upon one's seeing it. In fact, the

FIGURE 54: Jampa Lhakhang Thongdrel

word "thongdrel" actually means "that which liberates upon seeing." In this case, the "liberation" refers to becoming free from the suffering caused by the five poisons of the mind: hatred, attachment, ignorance, pride, and jealousy. Simply looking upon the enlightened beings pictured in the work of art is deemed to extend their awareness to the viewer. The sacred dances themselves are considered a form of thongdrel—liberation through seeing—for they are embodied mandalas of the deities and their divine qualities.

Brain Science and "Liberation through Seeing"

I had been struck since first encountering this notion of a spiritual transformation accomplished by seeing something, and more so, by looking at dance in particular. We now know from scientific research that the architecture of the brain responds to and alters itself through the mere viewing of dance. In *Dancing to Learn: The Brain's Cognition, Emotion, and Movement*, dance anthropologist Dr. Judith Lynne Hanna articulates the vast and complex relationship between dance and the phenomenon of neuroplasticity, the brain's ability to adapt and reorganize itself in response to new information. Simply by observing movement, we generate new brain cells that connect to growing neural networks—thereby improving cognition. Hanna explains that in the evolutionary process "attention to motion is critical for survival to cope with eating or being eaten, social bonding."[26]

In addition to this amazing network of interconnections, research shows that mirror neurons in the premotor cortex of the brain activate when performing an action *and* when observing the same action performed by another. This demonstrates how we catalyze empathy—that is, the ability to identify with or understand another person's feelings or condition. Neuroscientist V. S. Ramachandran, in his TED Talk "The Neurons that Shaped Civilization," asserts, "Mirror neurons dissolve the barrier between you and someone else." This comment reflects the cornerstone of Buddhist philosophy—there is no separate, inherent self; we exist only as a result of interdependent causes, conditions, and relationships. This organic reality in our brain is what the Buddhist teachings, highly refined meditations, and sacred dances seek to nurture, build upon, and map onto the greater social fabric. We humans are biologically wired to be moved to empathy by watching dance. How did the ancient Buddhist masters know?

Setup for the Consecration

People had come from near and far to Jampa Lhakhang for the day of rituals. Red-robed monks stood in attendance beside a couple of tables located in front of the thongdrel. Draped in yellow print fabric, one of the tables held a multitude of offerings and the other served as an altar. The table of offerings was laden with pineapples, oranges, bananas, apples, whole tropical fruits, and neatly stacked boxes of fruit juice, while the main altar was overflowing with orchids, potted marigolds and chrysanthemums, vases filled with multicolor flower arrangements, sparkling brass bowls of water, and an arrangement of colorful torma. Throughout the morning, a steady stream of devotees made the requisite three prostrations to the head lama (always to the lama or guru first, as he is the conduit to the teachings of the Buddha) and then to the Buddha Maitreya pictured in the thongdrel. Others, spinning prayer wheels and repeating sacred mantras, circumambulated the temple.

The Jampa temple had never had a thongdrel. The tapestry had been commissioned three years earlier and funds were raised for the project, which took two years to complete. As this was a first for the community, it would certainly enhance the upcoming festival and many more for years to come.

A sense of the sacred is always within reach in this landscape, abundant with fluttering prayer flags, temples, *stupas* (reliquary structures), and even Buddhist shrines in most private homes. It is, therefore, customary to consecrate any Buddhist image, large or small, with an elaborate ritual—to invite the deities and wisdom beings into the objects and seal their presence. This is done so the sacred objects can bestow blessings and merit upon those who venerate them.

Inside a white tent, the orchestra of orange-robed monks with tall, red ceremonial hats sat on the ground beating their round, blue hand drums with hooked sticks. The deep hypnotic drone of the chant master and the blasts of the six-foot-long dungchen, along with the clouds of incense smoke, stirred my senses away from the mundane and sent me into another realm.

Conversation with the Chakar Champon

I was brought back to earth when Chakar Lam Dorje's eldest son Tenzin pulled up some chairs behind the orchestra tent for a conversation. A truly gifted dancer, Tenzin demonstrated his genuine interest in dancing the cham when he was just 10 years old. At the time, he began mingling with the older dancers and learning some of the steps. By age 12, he was seriously training to know and perform the dances and by 16, he was designated champon. An integral link in the lineage, he has been the master dancer for 38 years and now functions as the executive producer of the drub. I was not surprised when I learned that he performs the Geb Ap Atsara role (the lead jester who acts as the program host—performing throughout the drub and managing the entire lineup). He, too, has been training his own son in the cham and the details of managing the event. Throughout the next few days of the drub, Tenzin's son seemed to be wherever I looked—making sure everything fell into place as it should.

Tenzin admitted it was a challenge integrating the new dance volunteers each year. He explained that after he teaches the newcomers the dances, he sends them to the nearby Jakar Dzong to gain experience dancing in another festival. Their rehearsal for the Jampa Lhakhang Drub is limited to two hours a day for two to four weeks before the event. I asked what he did the rest of the year. He replied that he, like his father, is a farmer. This is true for most of the dancers—which is why they don't reliably show up for rehearsals that interfere with their livelihood.

As the sounds of crashing cymbals, blaring horns, and beating drums signaled the beginning of a sacred dance, I squeezed in one last question, "What makes a good dancer?" The champon gave the response of a wise master: "Practice!"

Double Thongdrel

We followed the sound cues to the cleared dance space before the great thongdrel in order to behold the expelling cham, *Tra Geg*. In this ritual, it is again evident how the Bhutanese are deeply connected with the notion that dance was our first language, and they employ it to express their most fundamental ideas. In this case, in an embodied purification ritual, they are driving away negativity and contamination from a newly created sacred object.

The *zhugdrel*, a ritual multicourse meal of butter tea, fried rice, lentils, boiled safflower, fruit, and *doma* (betel nut and lime paste preparation)—all served by monk novices to the presiding monks, musicians, dancers, and community benefactors—continued for a very long time. Although enjoyed by the human participants, the zhugdrel is intended and visualized first as an offering to the celestial beings to ensure the success of an endeavor.

The morning ceremonies concluded with a famous sacred dance, *Dramitse Nga Cham*.

So, yes, it was a most lucky day or, as the Bhutanese would say—auspicious. I had the unexpected thrill of viewing cham before a magnificent thongdrel—a double thongdrel! And I could now anticipate this double sighting again on the final day of the drub.

 ## Tra Geg

At the four corners of the space in front of the great thongdrel, stand four bare-chested dancers in orange, above-the-knee, tiger-skin skirts and red, wrathful masks crowned with five skull figures. Each dancer holds a torch consisting of a bundle of burning sticks in one hand and carries a bag slung over a shoulder containing a powder they throw on the lit torches to keep them aflame. They leap around, swoop their torsos in arcs from side to side, and shake their heads back and forth to the insistent blasts of the long horns. This *mecham* (fire dance) called *Tra Geg* (pronounced Tra-gyeh) clears away contamination and defilement. "Tra" means enemy and "Geg" means negative spirit.

This dance of expelling obstacles and negativity is believed to have been originally introduced by Guru Rinpoche and later rediscovered as a tercham revelation. *Tra Geg* is performed specifically at consecration ceremonies for new temples, statues, paintings, stupas, or any new construction.

The four dancers represent the guardian deities of the four cardinal directions. According to Khenpo Tashi, this cham ritual is included at consecration ceremonies to remove contamination from the ego, pride, or attachment the artists, builders, or sponsors may have imparted upon the project.[27]

Once the negativity has been driven out by means of the dance, a head monk performs a purification rite, pouring saffron water from a ritual ewer and invoking blessings from the enlightened beings for the newly constructed object. You can view a similar fire dance *Geg-toe Mecham* at https://digitalcollections.nypl.org/items/61268fe0-8292-0130-03a6-3c075448cc4b.

Dramitse Nga Cham (DRUM DANCE OF DRAMITSE)

The droning horns and steady rhythm set by the cymbals usher in the 16 animal-masked dancers led by the dancer wearing a mask of the snow lion. With dynamic energy, one by one, each dancer bounds into the dance space and begins spinning and swooping his torso in arcs. After each dancer makes his spirited entrance, he joins the circle of already-present dancers who are moving quietly in the background until all the dancers have joined the circle. The dance proceeds in 21 sections alternating between calm movements evoking peaceful deities and athletic moves representing wrathful ones. Between each section the leader shouts *"Phat"*—a Tibetan syllable vocalized as a reminder to halt all dualistic thinking.

For this cham, the dancers wear yellow, swishy skirts made of multiple-layered kerchiefs gathered at the waistband and carry a drum (*nga*) in their left hand and a hooked stick in their right (except for the snow lion, who carries cymbals). They perform their steps while beating the drum of dharma for all to hear and have a skillful way of flipping the drum this way and that before each drumbeat. *Dramitse Nga Cham* is considered to be a treasure dance, envisioned during the meditation of Kunga Gyeltshen (also known as Kunga Wangpo), a great treasure revealer during the 15th century. It is recognized by UNESCO as a Masterpiece of Intangible Cultural Heritage. See it for yourself at https://digitalcollections.nypl.org/items/f15ae620-e511-0130-0058-3c075448cc4b.

CHAPTER TWELVE

The Jampa Lhakhang Drub

OPENING CEREMONIES

WE ARRIVED at the courtyard of the Chakar Lama's temple around midday, as the officiants and dancers were gathering for preliminary rituals before the Procession of the Relics. We looked up at the sky and marveled at the rainbow that had formed around the sun—an auspicious sign I was told. I was greeted by Chakar Lam Dorje and Tenzin as they emerged from the Lama's house dressed in their tshechu best, draped in ceremonial *kabney* of reddish-orange for the Lama and fuchsia for Tenzin—colors identifying their status and role. The monks from Buli Monastery (located in the nearby Chume Valley) were present as they would preside over the ritual aspect of the drub, being co-practitioners of the Dorje Lingpa tradition. Next to an ornamental parasol that rested against the temple wall, two young monks rehearsed on the *jaling* (oboes). The female folk dance performers arrived decked out in colorful kira and coordinated toego. They all proceeded into the temple and awaited the last-minute arrival of the male dancers who straggled in while still adjusting their ceremonial gho.

Once the temple ceremony was completed, the oboes sounded as the officiants and performers descended the temple steps, now attired in special ceremonial hats and bearing banners, a parasol, sacred statues, and relics. Amidst the smoke from the burning incense, they formed a circle in the courtyard for a *marchang* offering. This is typically included at Bhutanese occasions and ceremonies (see chapter 6) to invoke the lamas, deities, celestial beings, and guardians of the four directions and eight cremation grounds to remove all obstacles to the accomplishment of the event. The chang is proffered from a small wine cauldron with three horns carved from ivory, wood, or butter decorating the lip. The officiant stands behind the cauldron, arms uplifted— left palm facing upward and the right hand holding the wine-filled ladle. He dips and offers up the ladle repeatedly as he chants a prayer and *visualizes* the alcohol as an extraordinary offering of five spiritual nectars.

Afterward, they proceeded out the gate and down the road with whoops and hollers, the monk musicians beating drums and blowing horns. Villagers, lining the route to Jampa Lhakhang, bowed to receive blessings from the

FIGURE 55: The Chakar Lama emerges from the temple to procession to the Jampa Lhakhang Drub.

treasure relics—initially blessed by Guru Rinpoche, then hidden, and later discovered by Dorje Lingpa for the benefit of future generations.

The procession entered the Jampa Temple gate, formed a circle outside the temple, and performed the marchang offering again. The dancers entered the temple courtyard and repeated the marchang offering a third time before at last they entered the temple, placed the relics within, made their prostrations, and took their seats for the zhugdrel that was part of this series of rituals. I stood in the temple courtyard listening to the uninterrupted ring of spinning prayer wheels that were turned by the continuous circuit of the faithful walk-

FIGURE 56: Lining up for the Procession of the Relics to Jampa Lhakhang

FIGURE 57: Procession to Jampa
Lhakhang (Monks)

.

FIGURE 58: Procession to
Jampa Lhakhang (Tenzin
bearing the phallus)

FIGURE 59: Marchang offering outside Jampa Lhakhang

FIGURE 60: Taking places for preliminary ritual at Jampa Lhakhang

147

ing around the temple. After the meal, the Offering Master, Chimi Rinzin (a younger son of Chakar Lam Dorje), gave the performers the obligatory pre-festival *tsoktam* (briefing) about the mental attitude they should bring to the drub and their performance.

Tenzin informed me that, around the age of eight, his younger brother, Chimi, was sent off for a monastic education to learn to perform the religious rituals, sacred musical instruments, and recitation of Buddhist texts. The Chakar Lama had planned this so that Chimi could eventually become the Drub Offering Master, ensuring there would be a family member trained to perform the religious aspects of the tradition just as Tenzin was entrusted to carry on the cham tradition. Once Chimi had acquired this knowledge, he left the monastery and became a lay monk (gomchen) to enable him to marry and continue his bloodline. For several years now, he has been serving as caretaker lama of the Nabji Temple—again, to fulfill the responsibility of the Chakar family to maintain the Nabji Drub and Temple—also a seat of the Dorje Lingpa tradition.

After the tsoktam, Chimi Rinzin gave each performer a blessing with holy water from the sacred ewer. The group exited the temple and the drub began.

Creating a Sacred Space

The events of the first day and night of the drub are dedicated to establishing the sacred space and then purifying the environment for the drub. The monks were joined by four masked dancers holding pine branches in a ritual of delineating and claiming the sacred ground. They and plenty of onlookers set off to each of the four corner stupas of the temple grounds. I was told this was to mark the area and signal to the evil spirits not to enter—just as landowners fence their land to demarcate the boundary. We completed this circumambulation in front of the temple where a small torma effigy (representing hostile forces) had been placed in a pit dug in the ground where a flagstone had been removed. This small, human-shaped, dough sculpture is one of several devices used during the course of the drub for the transference of negative elements such as evil and sickness from the community (both local and universal).

Once the torma is buried, the negativities are believed to be eliminated during the festival and until the ritual is performed again at the next festival. The informal name for this ritual is *torma phang*, meaning to bury, castaway, or destroy the torma.

Meanwhile in the dance performance space marked off in a courtyard by a large chalk circle, the *chamjug* (dance rehearsal) was already taking place. The dancers—dressed, not in their costumes, but in plain, billowing white skirts worn over their gho—performed two cham in this symbolic open rehearsal.

The monks had by now reentered the temple for a lengthy prayer cycle.

FIGURE 61: Circumambulation of the temple grounds at Jampa Lhakhang

FIGURE 62: Torma burial ritual at Jampa Lhakhang

FIGURE 63: (Opposite) Chamjug—Public dance rehearsal at Jampa Lhakhang

Their chanting, horn playing, and drum beating could be heard over the loud-speaker system. Concurrently, the dance rehearsal was accompanied with live cymbals and horns. The two soundtracks overlapped each other in a compound layering of spiritual sound.

FIRST NIGHT RITES

Activities stopped for a few hours so people could eat dinner in time to reconvene at the temple grounds after dark at about 9:30 P.M. The number of

attendees had hugely increased as neighboring villagers and tourists from all over poured into the area for the infamous first night program of the Jampa Lhakhang Drub. When we arrived at the courtyard dance space, a bonfire had been built in the center and the atsaras were clowning around with each other and interacting with many of the attendees. The November night air was quite chilly as the temperature drops dramatically once the sun begins to set. Seated on the cold flagstones around the dance space, we felt the chill permeate deep into our bones as we awaited the *jinsek* (fire ritual). In Vajrayana Buddhism, jinsek is a category of ritual performance that uses fire as the agent for conveying offerings to the gods as well as purging negativity.

Suddenly, drums, cymbals, and horns introduced *Zhanag Phur Cham* (Black Hat Dance with Phurba [ritual dagger]). The deep darkness of the night, lit only by the bonfire and occasional sparks shooting skyward, added a new dimension of mystery to this powerful, danced ritual performed in tantric dress with an apron featuring the image of a fierce deity and the round black hat topped with a mirror, skull figure, and peacock feathers. The spinning, arcing, and dipping of the monk dancers in their full, brocade robes with long, floppy sleeves appeared as impressionistic paintbrush strokes of color flecked against the dark, nighttime canvas. This rite is performed to purify the ground. It is believed to do so by pacifying the malevolent beings in order to take possession of the site from them.

The Black Hat dancers paused in a large circle around the bonfire as horns, cymbals, screeches, and whistles announced four *ging* (powerful, benevolent forces that dispel obstacles) as they danced a spirited entrance into the circle. Wearing short, tiger-skin skirts, decorative collars over bare chests, and semi-wrathful masks, they formed an inner circle surrounding the bonfire. Attendants brought out a large paper effigy (drawing of a body on a rectangular piece of handmade paper) tied atop four poles. Each of the ging held a pole so that the effigy, symbolic of negative forces, was suspended aloft directly above the blazing fire. Inside the musician's pavilion, the monks intoned a rhythmic formula to the beat of a drum. Keeping time with the escalating speed of the chant, attendants entered the dancers' circle and distributed chang, grains, and other offering ingredients by filling the small brass cups the Black Hat dancers held in their hands. The dancers then tossed the offerings to the earth spirits while the attendants ran back inside the pavilion to get more supplies, quickly returned to the dancers, and replenished the dancers' cups for another round. This was repeated over and over with an increasingly urgent tempo.

Deep horn blasts punctuated each section of the dance. An assistant lama carried a black, triangular box containing the *linga* (a small dough effigy into which negative forces and obstacles are summoned) and placed it on the ground. Attendants brought out various ritual implements (phurba, fan, chain, hook, bell) for the lead dancer to use to symbolically subdue, and ultimately liberate, the negative forces by cutting up the linga. With the arrival of each new implement, the dancers initiated a new round of dancing. The building drama culminated with a display of pyrotechnics when a Black Hat dancer tossed a mixture of wild berry oil and grain onto the fire, causing the flames and sparks to burst upward just as the paper effigy was lowered and completely consumed. The linga was also thrown into the fire.

This expurgatory rite was immediately followed by a moving expression of grace and humility. The Black Hat dancers exited the circle and Chimi Rinzin, in his red and orange lama robes holding a bunched-up, white khata, danced *Tsogcham*, a dance of offering in which the destroyed negative forces within the linga are offered to the multitudes of deities in an imaginary, visualized feast. Sometimes the participants also share in in the feast by partaking of a bit of torma or a crumb of bread. "*Tsog*" translates as "multitudes" or "accumulations" and is a tantric practice of generating (internally) a sense of offering. It is hoped that the divine hosts will then confer their power on the practitioners to overcome shortcomings and obstacles to enlightenment. *Tsogcham* is the danced expression of this concept and Chimi Rinzin's serene flow of generous spirals, torso dips, and sweeping turns was an inspired rendering of it. *Tsogcham* is an exceptional example of how much of cham occurs within the performer's mind—in essence, a dance of the mind.

I spoke with Chimi Rinzin the next day to learn what kind of mental preparation he does in order to perform such a stirring invocation. With cham, the performance preparation is mental, not physical. Chimi Rinzin explained that he meditates on the three roots—*Lama-Yidam-Khandro*—to cultivate the

FIGURE 64: Ging hold the paper effigy above the fire during the jinsek (Jampa Lhakhang)

mental attitude to perform this dance. In the Nyingma tradition, practitioners take spiritual refuge in this formulation, conceived to aid one's progress toward enlightenment:

1) Lama—one's guru, who is considered a personification of the Buddha and one's guide to attaining enlightenment
2) Yidam—the practitioner's meditational deity; symbolically representative of the qualities of the Buddha and the guru
3) Khandro—a protector and facilitator of the teachings of Buddhism

When I asked Chakar Lam Dorje if he also performed *Tsogcham*, his eyes twinkled as he waggled his head. "It was the first dance I learned," he replied.

THE FIRE ARCH

Once *Tsogcham* was completed, the swollen throngs of attendees moved together from the courtyard out to an open field in the rural darkness. There a huge arch of pine wood strung with kindling branches had been constructed for the *Mewang* (fire offering). In one of the dramatic highlights of the festival, the arch was set ablaze. This is done, again, to purify the earth possessed by negative spirits. It is customary to run through the burning arch as an act of ritual cleansing. Khenpo Tashi explained that in former times attendees enacted this ritual with strong faith and a pure heart as the burning arch represents the light of wisdom that burns away mental delusion. Nowadays it has become such a mobbed tourist spectacle that it is difficult to perceive the original motivation.

Another big attraction of the first night of the festival at Jampa Lhakhang is the *Naked Dance*, which traditionally is performed around midnight. We arrived back at the temple dance ground after the fire offering at about 11:30 P.M., just as they were announcing that the *Naked Dance* would commence at 12:30 A.M. The dancers launched into several cham and 12:30 became 1:30. The crowd was restless and the night air was cold. The extra police hired for the evening warned that no photography or recording would be allowed during the *Naked Dance* out of respect for the dance and the dancers. Should the police even see a phone or camera, it would be confiscated. This is strictly enforced—especially because people are free to photograph and video all the other dances during the festival and are accustomed to posting them on social media sites.

The dance is sometimes called *Yulim Cham* and sometimes just *Tercham* because it is a tercham (treasure dance). According to Chakar Lam Dorje, the dance was first performed in the town of Nabji in the Trongsa district (where Guru Rinpoche negotiated the peace between King Sindhu Raja of Bumthang and the Indian King Nawoche). In the familiar Himalayan Buddhist trope, a band of obstructive spirits was impeding the progress of a nearby temple-building project. They destroyed whatever had been constructed each day. And, as is often the case, a dance dispels the obstacles and paves the way for the flourishing of Buddhism. Dorje Lingpa envisioned the tercham as a distraction tactic to enable the building of the temple. He later introduced the dance at Jampa Lhakhang in Bumthang, when he consecrated the temple there.

The bonfire was rekindled and finally the tercham dancers (a minimum of seven, but usually between 15 and 20 dancers depending on availability of volunteers) rushed out of the *chamkhang* (green room)* and formed a circle around the dancing flames. The completely naked male dancers, wearing only a white stocking mask with eyes cut out (to hide their faces), stood bending and taunting in a provocative show of their nudity. The dance did not include the usual cham movements. Instead, the majority of the dancers maintained a circle around the fire while solo dancers, duos, and trios took turns skipping off from the circle and lunging toward the audience in a tantalizing exhibition of their sexual organs; they then returned to the circle and the fire to warm their exposed bodies. Indeed, the dance enacted what the Chakar Lama had related to me—an anecdote of how the dancers of *Tercham* distracted the obstructive spirits by exhibiting their memorable, oddly shaped sexual organs. Khenpo Tashi, however, interprets the dance as a portrayal of naked awareness—the pure nature of our minds. Himalayan Buddhism has a history of using the literal naked body to represent spontaneous wisdom and clarity unconstrained by conventional limitations. In many sacred biographies, it is common to read about highly accomplished yogis or yoginis who eschew clothing and practice either naked or in rags. So, Dorje Lingpa is not the only Buddhist saint who had these unorthodox views and practices.

The cham is performed to the traditional sacred dance accompaniment of drums and cymbals and lasts about 45 minutes. It is a very different notion of dance that is sacred. But then again, in Tantra, any action born of a pure

---

*The chamkhang is usually located inside the temple or monastery; but at Jampa Lhakhang, there is a dedicated small, separate structure.

motivation to serve others and alleviate suffering is considered "skillful means." And so the profane *becomes* sacred.

The Bhutanese observers seemed very enthusiastic about *Tercham* and encouraged their little ones to stay awake for it.

TSUKTON (BEGINNING)

The second day of the festival began with the cham called *Shinje Yab-Yum* (Dance of the Lord of Death and His Consort).

In contrast to the physically connected artistic depictions of yab-yum, or coupled, tantric deities, this duet features two parallel figures that spin, hop, and jump while slicing through the air with their swords. Only occasionally do they even dance facing each other.

Many of the usual cham from the evening before were repeated throughout the day. The high point of the afternoon was the performance of a rather unique Dorje Lingpa tercham called *Jachung Boechung* (Dance of the Two Mythical Birds). Chakar Lam Dorje narrated the story of this dance-play when I interviewed him at his home prior to the festival.

After a dinner break, as darkness descended, we returned to find the temple courtyard eerily empty except for a gaggle of little ones left on their own and burning off some excess energy in the Lama's viewing pavilion. Finally, people started regathering and a bonfire was lit. The clanging of cymbals ushered in *Droe Cham*, a Dorje Lingpa tercham of *Guru Dragpo*—a wrathful emanation of Guru Rinpoche.

The nighttime program ended with a repeat performance of the *Naked Dance*.

BARTON (MIDDLE)

I arrived at the dance courtyard on the third morning and engaged Sonam Pede in a brief conversation despite her busy performing schedule that day. Sonam has led the women folk dancers for three years now, although, she explained that they work as a team in deciding which dances to perform and

Text continues on page 161 ▶

Shinje Yab-Yum (DANCE OF THE LORD OF DEATH AND HIS CONSORT)

This dance often opens tshechu programs as another means of expelling negative spirits and consecrating the environs. Shinje is a wrathful emanation of Manjushri, the Deity of Wisdom. In the dance he and his consort each carry the transmutative sword that cuts through attachment and transforms ignorance into wisdom, greed into generosity, and

FIGURE 65: *Shinje Yab-Yum* (Jampa Lhakhang)

anger into lovingkindness. They dance wearing long brocade dresses and red buffalo masks with sharp, upcurling horns. "*Yab-yum*" is a Tibetan word meaning "father/mother" and represents the male/female union of compassion and wis- dom that, together, eliminate ignorance and deluded thinking. See it for yourself at https://digitalcollections.nypl.org/items/39fc1680-8292-0130-8840-3c075448cc4b.

Jachung Boechung (Dance of the Two Mythical Birds)

This dance-play tells the story of Boechung, the illegitimate son of Princess Ashe Jaza (Chinese princess betrothed to Tibetan King Songtsen Gampo) and the god Jajin (Indra—king of the gods in Hindu mythology). The princess lost her way as she traveled from China to Tibet to meet her betrothed. Jajin encountered the lost princess and left her with child. As she was determined to marry the king of Tibet, she abandoned the child (Boechung). Alone on a mountaintop, Boechung is attacked by two *jachung* (garudas, or mythical birds). Jajin sends atsaras to rescue Boechung. The child's unresponsiveness prompts them to exhaust all means to save him. They consult an astrologer; they perform a torma ritual to ransom his life; a *pawo* (healer) tries various methods. Finally, the father must call a doctor and a monk to cure his son. Tenzin played all three demanding roles of jester, Jajin (father), and pawo. By the end, Boechung is saved. He jumps up from the supine position he has maintained throughout the dance and runs offstage. Afterward, the father and healer ride off together on horseback (astride a pole). The dance is intended to chase away evil spirits and establish peace and harmony within the family and community. (See photo on next page.)

 ## Droe Cham (Wrathful Dance)

The dancers wear monks' brocade costumes and wrathful masks as they perform this dance to drive away evil spirits and then make a fruit offering. The dance builds to a climax when all of the dancers, stretching their arms sideward with palms uplifted, form a circle around the bonfire. In a heart-stopping moment, they jump up in unison throwing their arms upward in a sublime, coordinated gesture of offering.

FIGURE 66: *Jachung Boechung* (Pawo performing a healing ritual for Boechung)

assembling the choreographic arrangements. These dances are not cham, but are part of Bhutan's folk dance traditions—some of which are almost 400 years old.

Sonam started dancing at the age of 17. Nowadays, her son and daughter are both involved in performing dances for school and community events. Sonam plans for her daughter, who is 13 and already a talented dancer, to replace her as the family dance volunteer at next year's drub.

The morning's program launched with a wine offering/fertility rite that is

FIGURE 67: Folk dance volunteers performing a boedra (Jampa Lhakhang)

particular to the Jampa Lhakhang Drub. First the *Zhanag Phur Cham* (Black Hat Dance with Phurba) was danced with Chimi Rinzin performing as tantric master. Even if I hadn't recognized his exquisite movements, I knew it was him when his little son walked over during a period of stillness and began playing with the back of his robes. This highlights a noteworthy quality of the tshechu atmosphere. Parents and elders do not require children to sit still and quietly through the proceedings. There is an easy manner in which the children feel free to move about and even walk up to or follow a dance character that sparks

FIGURE 68: *Zhanag Phur Cham* (Jampa Lhakhang)

their curiosity. Occasionally the little boys (remember, the cham dancers are male) experiment with some of the dance steps on the sidelines. Parents and monks do not interfere with this behavior, even if the children seem to get in the way of a dancer. Sometimes an older sibling is sent to recover a wandering toddler. But this cultural legacy belongs to each succeeding generation and this is how it is absorbed—in body, speech, and mind.

After their initial dance, the Black Hat dancers stood in a semicircle, while the skeleton dancers entered the dance ground carrying a black cloth and

FIGURE 69: *Zhanag Phur Cham* (Jampa Lhakhang)

triangular black box containing the linga that they placed on the ground in the center. The four skeleton dancers performed *Durdag Cham* (Lords of the Cremation Grounds Dance), with its deep backbends and shaking skeleton fingers, and then exited. Now with the linga in place, the Black Hat dancers resumed their spinning steps around it until the tantric master bent over and severed the linga with his phurba in an act of liberation. (Wrathful actions are

executed with compassionate intention—as in a parent's stern behavior toward a child about to wander into a dangerous situation.)

Once this sequence was completed, the Black Hat dancers remained present while the female folk dancers, carrying brass offering bowls of chang, entered and formed a horizontal line. Dressed as the Old Man Atsara, Tenzin presided over the fertility rite. He carried a giant papier-mâché phallus with special relics and herbs inserted. He explained to me later that first he performs the wine-offering ceremony to the deities, presenting wine to them to ensure the

FIGURE 71: *Durdag Cham* (Jampa Lhakhang)

prosperity of the community. Indeed, as I had observed, he dips the phallus into the wine urn and sprinkles it very liberally over everything in its path, and then he taps the forehead of everyone who lines up for a fertility blessing. He guarantees its effectiveness for the coming year—as does Chakar Lam Dorje. When we were watching the dances earlier, the Lama recounted to me many of the ritual's success stories and kindly inquired if I would like to receive a fertility blessing.

FIGURE 72: Tenzin performing the annual fertility rite (Jampa Lhakhang)

Unseen Dance—An Essential Component of Ritual

That afternoon, while the cham program continued, I asked the Chakar Lama about the special ritual cycle that was occurring inside the temple. I wanted to know more about this "unseen" ritual—also a Dorje Lingpa terma—that was simultaneously taking place. I was interested in the role of dance (also unseen by the public) within this sacred rite. A theological elucidation of the proceedings is beyond my scope of scholarship. However, I have since learned that this is considered an extremely powerful ritual and is carried out annually in all of the dzongs in the country. There are also a number of published accounts of similar rituals performed in exiled Tibetan monasteries in India.[28]

The Lama motioned for me to come along, and I followed him across the campus to the temple entrance. The monks had already been performing the prayers for a couple of hours by the time we entered. Just as everyone else did, the 88-year-old Lama removed his shoes (felt monks' boots) while standing in the entryway and capably performed his prostrations without any assistance. Chakar Lam Dorje then seated himself on his prayer cushion to the right of the presiding lama from Buli Monastery.

Gradually, all of the Chakar Lama's extended family and the dancers showed up and patiently performed a choreography of prostrations in what seemed like a human weaving of overlapping bodies in the narrow and tight temple space. They took their places on the floor for this sacrosanct ritual—*Guru Dragpo Tordo*—that they perform for the benefit of the community. As mentioned before, Guru Dragpo is a wrathful emanation of Guru Rinpoche (the *drag* in Dragpo means "ferocity" and refers to the fierce energy summoned by Guru Rinpoche to subdue and fend off obstacles to Buddhism and enlightenment). According to one of the monks from Buli, this particular practice is from a Dorje Lingpa terma revealed at *Taktsang* (Tiger's Nest) in Paro, Bhutan. In preparation for this expelling ritual, the monks had constructed three large torma according to exact specifications in the terma text. The torma were sitting on trays and placed on the altar in the center of the temple.

The monks were seated on the floor intoning a rhythmic incantation that they read from the horizontal tablets, flipping over the completed pages of scripture onto a separate pile. At each pause in the recitation, the monk musicians would produce a flood of sound with cymbals and blasts from the thighbone trumpets and long horns. The sonic intensity and concentrated smoke and scent from the incense were quite stirring. Then the music would cease and the monks resumed the recitation to the insistent beat of the large drums.

FIGURE 73: Torma for the *Torgyab* ritual (Jampa Lhakhang)

It grew dark outside and we all transitioned to the interior courtyard of the temple. The three torma were brought out of the temple and set on a bench. They were substantial, pyramidal dough sculptures made of specified symbolic ingredients, painted with faces, and covered with inserted colored flags, miniature painted cardboard signs, money, and colored sticks. These torma are constructions for trapping negative forces, which are then offered to the deities in exchange for the community's well-being.

The monks came out wearing their tall ceremonial hats and the lead lama wore the robe of a Tantric Black Hat master as did several other monks. Two

FIGURE 74: An officiating lama dressed in the Black Hat costume prepares to cast the torma into the fire.

of the community dancers were costumed as semi-wrathful ging in orange, tiger-skin skirts and they carried burning torches. Two other dancers wore Bhutanese, medieval, warrior attire (white skirt; decorated crossed collar; and tall, red, sheepskin hat).

The Offering Master, Chimi Rinzin, circulated through the group and carried a large bowl of dried grain from which we all took a generous handful. The monks performed more recitations to the command of the drum. At frequent intervals Chimi Rinzin cued everyone to throw some of the grains at the torma while we all shouted, "*Bhyo*," meaning "expel." We repeated this at quickening

FIGURE 75: *Torgyab* ritual
(Jampa Lhakhang)

intervals. The Black Hat dancer performed his dance before the torma. Then the trays of offering cakes were lifted and we proceeded in the darkness out to a field where a large bonfire was lit. Throughout this outdoor ritual, one of the dance volunteers periodically set off firecrackers. In a symbolic demonstration of exorcizing negativity and collective purification, several men lifted a tray as Chimi Rinzin recited a prayer and together they hurled the torma into the fire. This was repeated with great ceremony for the other two torma.

The Black Hat master danced, followed by the ging. Finally, the dancers costumed in traditional warrior attire performed *Beh*, the martial folk dance. They wielded the multicolored victory banner and shouted fierce whoops and war cries—a final tactic to chase away negative forces.

We moved on from the site and into the night in collective song intoning the haunting melody of a *legs-so* (traditional song of glorification and gratitude to the deities.)

* * * * *

I pause here to underscore that over the three previous days I had witnessed dances in which much of the "choreographed" activity takes place within the mind of the dancer. Other dances are intended to be performed unseen by a human audience (and not for personal pleasure). These concepts were challenging, reorienting, and expanding my notions of the mind-body relationship and potentialities for dance and its performance.

Jugton (Conclusion)

On the concluding day of the festival, the giant thongdrel was raised on the flagpoles where it had been initially consecrated only days before. The indigo, fuchsia, emerald, ruby, amethyst, and topaz jewel-toned figures against the aquamarine background provided a luscious backdrop to one of my favorite cham—*Pacham* (Dance of the Heroes and Heroines).

Although this dance is performed throughout Bhutan following the Pema Lingpa (Peling) vision of the choreography (see chapter 4), at Jampa Lhakhang they perform the Dorje Lingpa (Dorling) version. Tenzin asserts that the

Dorje Lingpa version has its own unique movement style. I would agree. The steps and overall sequencing of both are quite similar, but the Dorje Lingpa tradition has an earthier energy and more primitive quality. Performing these movements before this colossal mandala of color, the dancers of Jampa Lhakhang truly brought Zangtopelri, poetically described as "a limitless mandala of rainbow beams," to life.[29]

Afterward, a designated group of volunteers began lowering the thongdrel, carefully rolling it up, and wrapping it for storage until the next year. As we proceeded back to the dance courtyard, I noticed an endless line of attendees had formed, circling a huge field to enter the temple and receive blessings from the relics in a ceremony called *tenwang*.

This final day was packed with Dorje Lingpa dance treasures. I was ecstatic to witness these remarkable dances from this rare lineage. *Dorling Gi Cham*, a unique "heroes" dance, was performed wielding metal swords. This tercham was followed by another—*Dorling Nga Cham*.

The program concluded with the three-hour dance-drama *Bardo Raksha Mangcham* (Dance of the Judgment of the Dead). This tercham, imparting lessons on the *bardo*, is the same dance previously described in Chapter Four: Into the Mandala. The lead dancer, wearing the ox-headed (raksha) mask and acting as mediator for the trial, is the first to enter and remains onstage after everyone has exited. As a representation of Manjushri (Deity of Wisdom), he stays seated on a chair after the dancing has ended. At that point, all of the members of the community pay their respects to him by lining up, placing white khatas around his neck, and leaving monetary offerings on a platter.

By the end of this ritual, in the fading light of dusk, one could no longer make out any of the brilliant colors of the raksha's costume. Only the white silk scarves blowing in the Bumthang evening darkness were discernable.

FIGURE 76: (Opposite) Chimi Rinzin and attending monk prepare the altar for the thongdrel ceremony on the final day of the Jampa Lhakhang Drub.

Pacham (DANCE OF THE HEROES AND HEROINES)

This tercham portrays a vision of Zangtopelri—the Copper-Colored Mountain Paradise abode of Guru Rinpoche peopled with sages, deities, heroes, and heroines dancing and singing the teachings of Buddhism amidst shimmering rainbows. One must appreciate that in the Vajrayana context, heroes and heroines refer to spiritual champions, not earthly warriors. The dance is performed during the supplication prayer to Guru Rinpoche as a welcome to the Guru and his entourage.

The dancers wear the multicolor kerchief skirts typical in many Bhutanese cham. The five loose pieces of yellow silk fabric printed with red and green floral patterns are layered over four solid-color silk pieces (white, red, blue, and green) and held together as a skirt with a belt. Crowning the dancers' heads are five-pronged golden crowns with one of the syllables of the five buddha families on each prong or, alternately, one of the five dakini syllables on each prong. In the left hand, the dancers hold a bell symbolizing wisdom and emptiness. In the right, they hold a *damaru*—a small, two-sided hand drum with a bead at the end of a short leather strap that throbs as the wrist is rotated back and forth—that symbolizes waking up from ignorance. These instruments are sounded as part of the choreography. The dancers enter and exit with an impossible

FIGURE 77: (Opposite) *Pacham*— a danced vision of Zangtopelri (Jampa Lhakhang)

FIGURE 78 (Above): *Pacham* (Jampa Lhakhang)

FIGURE 79: *Pacham* (Jampa Lhakhang)

yarfar jump in which they fold their bodies forward, bringing their arms and straight legs together in the air. Khenpo Tashi says this represents "the gesture of a deity which is active and vibrant for the sake of other beings."[30] I have also heard him say that it signifies the merging of wisdom and compassion. See it for yourself at https://digitalcollections.nypl.org/items/aad8ada0-e377-0130-e574-3c075448cc4b.[31]

FIGURE 80: *Pacham* (Jampa Lhakhang)

Dorling Gi Cham (SWORD DANCE)

This "heroes" dance, in the Dorje Lingpa tradition, is performed to the beat of the cymbals and a bell. The dancers are dressed in the yellow, gathered skirts; long-sleeved, colorful, silk shirts; and a decorated, crossed collar. They wear no masks, but wrap their heads in a fabric similar to headdresses worn by women of the Bumthang region. Some of the dancers also wear long, braided bangs attached to a headband that hang over their faces. This is done to disguise themselves from recognition by negative forces. The ten dancers form a

FIGURE 81: *Dorling Gi Cham*—Sword Dance (Jampa Lhakhang)

circle and make slicing motions with a sword held in the right hand, while the left hand performs mudras. Spinning one way and then the other, they move around in the circle. Eventually the free hand takes hold of the tip of the sword forming an enclosed circular shape. The arms continue their slices in a more limited range (due to the hand position) as the dancers move around the circle with knee lifts. The energy builds as the left hand releases the tip of the weapon and the sword movements expand into larger swoops while the traveling steps become airborne hops. The circle opens into a line and the dancers exit spinning out of the performance space. See it for yourself at https://digitalcollections.nypl.org/items/8c146410-e377-0130-4a5c-3c075448cc4b.

FIGURE 82: *Dorling Gi Cham* (Jampa Lhakhang)

FIGURE 83: *Dorling Gi Cham* (Jampa Lhakhang)

FIGURE 84: *Dorling Gi Cham* (Jampa Lhakhang)

Dorling Nga Cham (DRUM DANCE FROM THE DORJE LINGPA TRADITION)

This *nga cham*, or drum dance, has many similarities to *Dramitse Nga Cham* and begins in much the same way. After the entrance, the dancing picks up intensity until it builds to a signature climax in which the circle opens into a line. Beating their drums in a strong and defined rhythm that they repeat, the dancers arc their torsos and extended one leg forward and then the other. They rotate their forearm and flip the drum this way and that before each drumbeat. They repeat the sequence over and over as they gradually move the line forward. When they reach the front of the dance space, they spin backward in retreat. The drumbeating line of dancers

FIGURE 85: *Dorling Nga Cham*—Drum Dance (Jampa Lhakhang)

proceeds forward again—this time beating the rhythm from an impossible, deep, squatting position. The line propels itself forward with each repetition using a powerful leap while maintaining the deep squat.

Nga cham are very popular in the Bhutanese culture. The drum represents wisdom and the hooked drumstick signifies compassion so that each beat of the drum unites wisdom with compassion. The sound is made to liberate all beings from suffering. The dance is a victorious celebration over evil and suffering. See it for yourself at https://digitalcollections.nypl.org/items/691de390-e377-0130-3d01-3c075448cc4b.

FIGURE 86: *Dorling Nga Cham* (Jampa Lhakhang)

The Continuity of a Spiritual Tradition

The treasure I found in Bumthang was a family with an integral sense of identification with and existential responsibility to an ancient spiritual tradition *that involves dance*. This personal commitment inspires and challenges the entire community to come together with a substantial contribution of time, energy, and resources to maintain its ancient heritage of religious and folk traditions. These traditions connect the community to its geography, spiritual forbearers, each other, and the world at large. The traditions are performed with the fervent belief that they benefit the community and have a ripple effect outward to all beings—a human tapestry of good and generous intention.

Unable, or unwilling, to tear myself away from Jampa Lhakhang, I was drawn back to the temple grounds the morning after the conclusion of the festival. I admired the new multihued prayer flags that had been hoisted during the final day after the thongdrel had been lowered. I visited the chamkhang that was empty except for the dance masks at rest.

Tenzin's son was busy taking down the loudspeakers from the roof of the temple. Afterward, we followed him inside where the monks were ensconced in performing another prayer cycle in gratitude for the successful tshechu.

Chimi Rinzin sat in a corner on the floor cheerfully guiding the young monks from Buli Monastery through the lengthy recitations. They leaned in following his every word. With a little hand gesture, he cued a young monk when to beat the drum. Nearby, his very young son stood wearing a plastic animal mask. As the monks concluded the ceremony with loud repeated blasts of all the horns and a sonorous ringing of the temple bell, Chimi Rinzin's son broke out into a few extemporaneous cham moves. I followed the monks once again in procession to the four corners of the temple grounds, retracing the enduring footpath of the sacred, and then left the premises—the horn blasts and steady drumbeat reverberating in the air.

CHAPTER THIRTEEN

Happiness, A National Value

Before leaving the country, I stopped in the capital city of Thimphu where the citizens were in a flurry of preparations for the 60th birth anniversary of their previous king, His Majesty the Fourth Druk Gyalpo (Dragon King) Jigme Singye Wangchuck. The wise, benevolent, and innovative leader, who reigned from 1972 to 2006, brought Bhutan into the modern age by implementing such public policies as free education, free healthcare services, well-planned business development, Internet connectivity, and vigorous environmental protections. Then, in an unparalleled move, he launched the drafting of a constitution and shifted the country to democracy. He also abdicated the throne to his eldest son, King Jigme Khesar Namgyel Wangchuck. According to some, the king took this action because he did not want his son to be unexpectedly thrust into the role of leadership as he had been at age 16 when his father died suddenly.

However, the fourth king is probably most renowned for introducing the concept of Gross National Happiness (GNH)—the government policy that measures the growth and development of the country by the happiness and contentment of its people. As mentioned in chapter 4, the policy emerges from four priorities—equitable and sustainable development, protection of the environment, preservation and promotion of Bhutan's unique cultural heritage, and provision of good and responsive governance. Although GNH may sound like naïve utopianism, the concept of wise governance is not new in Bhutan. Buddhist societies have long held the tradition of the *dharmaraja*, a virtuous Buddhist king, also known as *cakravartin* (Sanskrit)—an ideal, universal ruler who governs ethically and benevolently over all subjects. In the seventh century, Emperor Songtsen Gampo (believed to have built the 108 Buddhist temples throughout the Himalayan region) instituted two enlightened codes of law—The Ten Virtuous Laws of Gods and The Sixteen Pure Laws of Mankind. He is regarded as the first dharmaraja of Tibet and is also considered to be a *bodhisattva* (selfless, enlightened being who dedicates himself or herself to helping others attain happiness). The British in India later used the title Dharmaraja in reference to those who held the supreme ruling position originated by Zhabdrung Ngawang Namgyal. The righteousness demanded of a Bhutanese ruler is apparent in Michael Aris's translation of the Bhutan Legal Code of 1729, which states, "As it is thus commanded, the custom of heaping good on good is instituted. The principal requirement of a king is the fair discharge of state law. Moreover . . . if a single king administers the law fairly he can bring his subjects to happiness in a single day. In general the reason for instituting state laws is for the very sake of the happiness of subjects."[32] So, there is historic precedent for and an expectation of the Bhutanese monarchy to dedicate itself to the well-being of the people, which helps explain how GNH would have organically developed in Bhutan.

I became aware of this enlightened approach and these political developments on my first trip to the country in February of 2011. At the same moment, in gaping contrast, the world was watching protests and struggle met by violence and repression as the Arab Spring ignited across the Arab world. I was struck by the wisdom of this Bhutanese monarch who was willing to let go of the reins of power for the greater good of the country—even before the populace desired the freedom or understood the tremendous responsibility of democracy.

In honor of the king's birthday, the entire country observed three days of celebration. Because Bhutan is a Buddhist country, prayers and rituals were woven into the festivities. The Je Khenpo, High Abbot and spiritual leader of the country, wrote a special *zhabten*—a prayer for the long life of an individual—composed by a senior spiritual figure whose power of speech is considered capable of turning words into reality. Other prayers and texts were to be recited across the country in dzongs, monasteries, temples, and seminaries. At Changlimithang Stadium in the capital city of Thimphu, 100 monks rehearsed a special cham called *Zheng Zhi Pem*—a gem of a dance exuding high energy. An elaborate ceremonial procession with military, monastic, and government officials, as well as an honor guard of 1,000 army personnel, was presented three times to His Majesty.

Because the people of Bhutan are so happy (more than 91 percent of the population were scored as happy in a 2015 GNH survey, see www.grossnation alhappiness.com), many of them wanted to participate in showing gratitude for His Majesty's leadership. The currency of gratitude in this land of happiness is *dance*. At the Royal Academy of Performing Arts, the artists rehearsed their own folk dance presentations inside the studio while, on the court outdoors, they directed a group of 138 bespectacled civil servants who showed up to learn and perform a dance for the king. Schools from all over the country prepared traditional folk dances as did a group of senior citizens.

FIGURE 87: Monks rehearsing *Zheng Zhi Pem* in Changlimithang Stadium (Thimphu). Photo credit: Michael Dottarar

Text continues on page 191 ▶

 ## Zheng Zhi Pem

Khenpo Tashi explains that "*zheng zhi*" means "get up and come along."[33] In this invocation to Guru Rinpoche, the dancers represent dakinis and twirl about in an offering of sublime beauty to invite the Guru's

presence. The common wisdom among champon and cham dancers is that cham is a most pleasing gift to invite and delight human and celestial beings alike. Hence, this invocatory dance is frequently performed at thongdrel ceremonies, public empowerments, and during private monastic ritual cycles held within the temple. The dancers wear the yellow kerchief skirts and richly colored silk-brocade jackets topped with a crossed dorje collar. They dance unmasked but wear

FIGURE 88: (Opposite) *Zheng Zhi Pem* performed as part of thongdrel ceremony at Trongsa Tshechu

FIGURE 89: (Below) *Zheng Zhi Pem* performed as part of thongdrel ceremony at Trongsa Tshechu

the five-pronged golden crowns with one of the five dakini syllables on each prong. In the left hand, the dancers hold a bell symbolizing wisdom and emptiness. In the right, they hold and rattle a damaru. See *Zheng Zhi Pem* at https://digitalcollections.nypl.org/items/62780cf0-8292-0130-c86e-3c075448cc4b.

FIGURE 90: *Zheng Zhi Pem* performed as part of thongdrel ceremony at Trongsa Tshechu

When one of the four queens called for 108 (the number that makes up a complete prayer cycle for Buddhists and is considered auspicious) women to volunteer to perform a dance, 200 turned out. The Bhutanese had readied multiple venues throughout the capital for all the events and entertainments, including a group of teenage hip hop dancers. The release of thousands of colorful, biodegradable balloons and three cake-cutting ceremonies were to cap the celebrations. But nothing could top the gift offered by His Majesty the fifth king—his announcement that Their Majesties were expecting the birth of a baby prince, heir to the Golden Throne and the continuity of the Druk

FIGURE 91: Civil servants rehearsing a dance for Fourth King's 60th birthday celebration at RAPA campus (Thimphu)

lineage. The royal announcement crowned the celebrations with a heightened dimension of national pride and hope.

Sure enough, during the Losar (New Year) holiday, the royal couple delivered the *gyalsey* (prince) at Lingkana Palace in Thimphu on February 5, 2016. To mark the much-anticipated national event, the Bhutanese people planted trees—108,000 saplings throughout the land—representing 108,000 prayers for the young prince. Each household planted a tree and thousands of volunteers turned out to plant more.

But planting trees is not simply Bhutan's gift to the baby gyalsey, it is an endowment for the future of our planet. In December of 2015, COP 21 (21st Session of the United Nations Conference of Parties on Climate Change held in Paris) brought together 195 nations plus the European Union to evaluate and make commitments to a global response to climate change and its impacts. From among all the parties to the conference, the tiny nation of Bhutan stood out because only Bhutan is carbon negative (its carbon footprint is less than neutral having a net effect of removing carbon dioxide from the atmosphere). This is achieved in part because the country's constitution mandates that a minimum of 60 percent of Bhutan's total land mass always remains under forest cover. In actuality today, 72 percent is forested. This government-imposed forest cover sequesters more than three times the carbon dioxide generated by the country, creating a net carbon sink (a system that absorbs carbon dioxide). In addition to the benefits of so much forest cover, Bhutan's chief export, hydroelectric power, offsets even more carbon, as it is renewable energy produced from the country's flowing rivers.

At COP 21, Bhutan recommitted to remain carbon neutral and has set high goals for itself, demonstrating a model for the greater community of nations. Just as Bhutan has concrete measures for sustaining quality of life in relationship to development, it has devised policies to ensure the country's carbon neutrality, such as preventing hunting, mining, and polluting in national forests; providing free electricity to rural farmers so they won't be forced to burn firewood for cooking; investing in sustainable transport and electric vehicles; aiming to grow 100 percent organic food by 2020; achieving zero waste by 2030; and yes, planting trees.

Bhutan's inspiring plan to fund its strong commitment to remain carbon neutral and how this plan could be replicated by other developing nations to finance their conservation pledges is enthusiastically explained in Prime Minister Tshering Tobgay's TED Talk entitled, "This Country Isn't Just Carbon Neutral—It's Carbon Negative." A devoted environmentalist myself, I could hardly contain my admiration for such staunch, governmental commitment to well-conceived environmental goals.

These events demonstrate that a government's focus on the happiness and well-being of its people, based on long-held customs of "heaping good on good," can be a powerful transformative force—an instrument for positive and reverberating social change. This may seem a far cry from sacred festivals and celebrations where everyone finds a way into the dancing; however, the holistic thinking that has led the Bhutanese to these progressive policies is part of the same spiritual perspective—Vajrayana Buddhism—that uses practices and expressions of mind *and body* to transform self and society into enlightened actors. This perspective is conceived as a dynamic delivery system for the flow of compassion toward all beings. It is a powerful concept—and why, when I saw their dances, I followed their footsteps into the mandala.

FIGURE 92: *Dramitse Nga Cham* (Trongsa Tshechu)

Epilogue

OF COURSE, I returned to Bhutan on a fifth trip. I went back to visit the Chakar Lama and his family, reconnect with old friends, and experience the dance traditions of another tshechu—Trongsa, the ancestral home of the royal family. Because the first two hereditary kings ruled the country from this mountainside location, Trongsa developed a highly regarded dance tradition—indeed, fit for royalty. The awesome dancing was perfectly framed by the majestic setting within the whitewashed Trongsa Dzong perched on a steep mountainside high above a deep gorge.

I finally got to see the men's folk dance I had learned during my early stint at RAPA—*Nub Zhey*! *Nub Zhey* is the traditional men's dance from the district of Trongsa. The dancers looked elegant in their bright-red skirts, blue jackets, and fabric head circlets.

One of the zhey dancers, Pelden Lhendup, explained that only a few years ago the *Nub Zhey* was on the verge of being forgotten. This became apparent in 2004 when the current king was to be installed as the 16th Trongsa *Penlop*. Penlop is the historic title given to the governors of Bhutan's main regions. It is royal tradition for the crown prince to serve as Trongsa Penlop before acceding to the throne—just as the first hereditary monarch of Bhutan Ugyen Wangchuck held the title before he was chosen to the throne. The performance of *Nub Zhey* is an integral part of the installation ceremony, but there were not enough dancers familiar with the song and the lengthy sequence of steps. For the Bhutanese, an endangered dance is akin to an endangered species of life and elicits an intervention. At the time, the *zheypon* (zhey dance leader) taught the dance to enough locals to adequately present at the ceremony.

FIGURES 93–96: Dancers from Trongsa perform their regional folk dance *Nub Zhey* at the Trongpa Tshechu.

FIGURE 93

FIGURE 94

Figure 95

Figure 96

Afterward, however, the Bhutan Broadcasting Service stepped in to create and air a television documentary to educate the public about the dance. The Trongsa District government furthered the revitalization effort by recruiting another group of men to learn the *Nub Zhey*. It was then that Pelden Lhendup learned the regional folk tradition and now has performed it continuously since 2014 at the Trongsa Tshechu. *Nub Zhey* is Trongsa's precious heritage and the people are proud to participate in its guardianship and performance. This is just another example of how dance is fundamental to Bhutanese culture—a living part of their identity.

One can only marvel at this culture's extraordinary dedication to its dances and appreciate the sense of purpose and connectedness that they engender. The dances of Bhutan are a genuine source of affirmation and transformation— individual, societal, and, by extension, universal. As part of every aspect of Bhutanese life, dance provides a way of knowing, understanding, and amplifying the lived and the aspirational experience.

Glossary

Achi Lhamo Tibetan folk operatic tradition attributed to 14th-century iron bridge building lama Thangtong Gyalpo

atsara masked jester or clown that performs at a tshechu

bardo the in-between state; period following one's death until the moment of conception in one's next life

Beh martial folk dance proclaiming victory over opposing forces

bodhi enlightened, awakened

bodhisattva an enlightened being who forgoes nirvana in this lifetime in order to devote himself/herself to helping all beings reach enlightenment

boedra Bhutanese folk dance form that was originally performed by court attendants

Bon indigenous, pre-Buddhist, animistic religion of the region

buddha awakened, or enlightened being

buddha nature essential pure nature and potential within all beings to attain enlightenment

cham Buddhist sacred dance

chamjug sacred dance rehearsal; assistant dance master

chamkhang green room (usually inside the temple or monastery)

champon sacred dance master

chang Bhutanese alcoholic brew

chu river; water

dakini Sanskrit word for emanation of feminine energy; wisdom facilitator in tantric Buddhist practice; khandro (Tibetan); "sky-dancer"

damaru small two-sided drum with a throbbing bead hanging from a short leather strap; used in rituals and sacred dance

deity yoga type of Vajrayana meditation in which the practitioner visualizes and meditates upon a deity in order to cultivate divine qualities and transcend human shortcomings; also called yidam yoga

desi secular ruler, or regent of the country

dharma Buddhist teachings, or religion

dharmaraja a righteous ruler; earthly bodhisattva, who protects the people and the Buddhist religion; cakravartin (Sanskrit)

doma Bhutanese treat of betel nut and lime paste wrapped in a banana leaf

dorje, dorji thunderbolt scepter used as a ritual implement; vajra (Sanskrit)

dramnyen Bhutanese seven-string lute

driglam namzha national values and etiquette

drub consecration

drubchen period of intense religious rituals held in a temple extending over several days; "great accomplishment"

Drukpa Kagyu principal sect of Buddhism in Bhutan and the official state religion

dungchen long, telescoping brass horns used in sacred music (can be made in different lengths)

dzong fortress/monastery complex built as a strategic stronghold in every major Bhutanese settlement

Dzongkha national language of Bhutan

dzongkhag district

five buddha families also Five Wisdom Buddhas; five qualities of enlightenment represented as five color-coded, directional buddhas in mandalic design

garuda mythical bird creature

gho Bhutanese men's national attire: knee-length, belted, wraparound, colorfully woven robe

ging benevolent deities that destroy obstacles

gomchen lay Buddhist practitioner; "great meditator"

gompa monastery

Gross National Happiness (GNH) government policy, conceived by the fourth king, that measures the growth and development of the country in relationship to the happiness and contentment of the people

guru (Sanskrit) teacher; master

gyalsey prince

Jampa (Tibetan) the Buddha of the Future; Maitreya (Sanskrit)

Je Khenpo highest religious official in the country

jinsek fire ritual

kabney men's ceremonial sash worn on formal occasions

karma the principle that every action (both good and bad) produces relative consequences within the cycle of continuity

khandro Tibetan word for dakini; female wisdom facilitator; "sky-dancer"

khata ceremonial white scarf given to a guest or person of stature as a sign of respect

khenpo abbot

kira women's traditional floor-length, straight, wraparound skirt

kuzuzampo la typical greeting that means "How are you?"

lama (Tibetan) Buddhist teacher and spiritual mentor; guru (Sanskrit)

Lemah men's folk dance performed during the Punakha Drubchen

lhakhang Buddhist temple

lim bamboo flute

linga dough effigy into which negative forces are summoned and then liberated through a symbolic sacrifice

Lingpa a suffix used to designate a terton, or treasure revealer

Mahakala a fierce deity and protector of the dharma; guardian deity of Bhutan who manifests as a raven

mahasiddi great mystic

Maitreya the great bodhisattva who is destined to manifest as the Buddha in a future age; Jampa in Tibetan

mandala cosmic diagram or blueprint of a divine palace used in tantric Buddhist meditation

mantra sacred syllables or phrases chanted to focus the mind during meditation as well as for their positive resonance

marchang an offering of alcohol or chang in tantric Buddhism

mecham fire dance

mewang fire offering

Mount Meru figurative axis of the universe in traditional Buddhist and Indian religious cosmology

mudras hand gestures used in Himalayan Buddhist prayer, meditations, and sacred dances

namthar sacred biography

nga drum

Nub Chu Sha Casting of the Relic ceremony performed at the Punakha Drubchen

Nyingma oldest school of Himalayan Buddhism

Nyingmapa followers of the oldest school of Himalayan Buddhism

pawo shaman; healer

pazap Zhabdrung Ngawang Namgyal's local Bhutanese militia

penlop historic title given to governors of the largest regions of Bhutan

phurba three-bladed ritual dagger

phurbu small version of a phurba

piwang two-string fiddle

raksha ox

Rangjung Kharsapani precious relic believed to have emerged from the cremated remains of the religious hierarch Tsampa Gyare

Rinpoche reincarnate lama; "precious"

shawo deer; stag

Shinje Lord of Death; a wrathful emanation of Manjushri, Deity of Wisdom

siddha accomplished mystic

stupa Buddhist reliquary structure

sutra Buddhist canonical scriptures that record the discourse of Buddha Shakyamuni

tantra Vajrayana texts that explicate philosophical principles and instructions for esoteric ritual and meditation practices

tercham revealed treasure dance

terma sacred treasures in the form of texts, artifacts, and visions understood to be hidden by Padmasambhava and his disciples during his lifetime for discovery in future times

terton discoverer of terma; treasure revealer

thongdrel giant appliqué tapestry featuring religious subjects; literally means "liberation upon seeing"

toego blousy, silk jacket worn by women

torgyab symbolic exorcism, in which elaborately decorated torma are cast into a fire and burned

torma ritual offering of flour and butter sculpted into intricate, multicolored forms made by monks

trulku reincarnated lama; the recognized rebirth of a previous exalted lama

tshechu sacred festival of dances and rituals held in honor of Padmasambhava

tsoktam briefing

vajra (Sanskrit) ritual scepter; thunderbolt; diamond; indestructible; dorje or dorji (Tibetan)

Vajrayana esoteric, apocalyptic style of Buddhism that emerged circa 500 C.E. in India and transplanted into the Himalayan region developing complex rituals and meditations to accelerate the realization of enlightenment or "Buddahood"

yab-yum (Tibetan) father-mother; refers to deities rendered in sexual union to signify the union of compassion (father) and wisdom (mother) present in the fully enlightened state

yangchen hammered dulcimer

yidam meditation deity; archetypal images that represent timeless enlightened qualities

yoga tantric Buddhist meditative practices that subtly coordinate mind and body in an effort to overcome ignorance and realize the interdependence of all beings; to "yoke" or "harness" one's energies and mind to meditation

yogi meditator; practitioner of Buddhist yoga

Zangtopelri the Copper-Colored Mountain Paradise of Guru Rinpoche

Zhabdrung honorific title meaning "at whose feet one submits"

zhey genre of traditional men's folk song/dance associated with spirituality and regional identity

zhugdrel a ceremony that, to cultivate a sense of auspiciousness, includes a symbolic meal of specified drinks and foods offered first to the divine beings, then to the honored guests, and finally to the rest of the participants

zhungdra genre of traditional women's folk song/dance from the 17th century

Notes

1. Joseph Goldstein, *Mindfulness: A Practical Guide to Awakening* (Boulder, CO: Sounds True, 2013), 43–77.

2. Robert A. F. Thurman, trans., "Background," in *The Tibetan Book of the Dead* (New York: Bantam Books, 1994), 18.

3. Robert Thurman, (lecture, Tibet House, New York City, September 13, 2017).

4. Joseph Goldstein, *Mindfulness: A Practical Guide to Awakening* (Boulder, CO: Sounds True, 2013), 368.

5. Quote provided by the Royal Office for Media of the Kingdom of Bhutan.

6. Robert Mayer, "Geographical and Other Borders in the Symbolism of Padmasambhava," Public talk given at the symposium "Moving Borders: Tibet in Interaction with Its Neighbors," Asia Society, New York, May 4–5, 2018, accessed November 23, 2018, https://www.academia.edu/37685631/Corrected_version_Geographical_and_Other_Borders_in_the_Symbolism_of_Padmasambhava.

7. Stephan Beyer, *The Cult of Tara: Magic and Ritual in Tibet* (Berkeley: University of California Press, 1978), 146–169.

8. Holly Gayley, introduction to *The Life and Revelations of Pema Lingpa*, by Pema Lingpa, translated by Sarah Harding (Ithaca, NY: Snow Lion Publications, 2003), 2.

9. Francoise Pommaret, "Dances in Bhutan: A Traditional Medium of Information," *Journal of Bhutan Studies* 14 (summer 2006): 26–35.

10. Khenpo Phuntshok Tashi, *Invoking Happiness: Guide to the Sacred Festivals of Bhutan and Gross National Happiness* (Independently published, 2011), 147.

11. Mona Schrempf, "Tibetan Ritual Dances and the Transformation of Space," *The Tibet Journal* 19, no. 2 (1994): 95–120.

12. René de Nebesky-Wojkowitz, *Tibetan Religious Dances* (New Delhi: Paljor Publications, 1997), 131–137.

13. Terry Ellingson, "Ancient Indian Drum Syllables and Bu Ston's Sham Pa Ta Ritual," *Ethnomusicology* 24 no. 3 (1980): 437.

14. Mona Schrempf, "Tibetan Ritual Dances and the Transformation of Space," *The Tibet .Journal* 19, no. 2 (1994): 106.

15. Jerome Robbins Dance Division, The New York Public Library, "Beh: Description," New York Public Library Digital Collections, 2005, http://digitalcollections.nypl.org/items/ffcad140-e7ef-0130-c08a-3c075448cc4b.

16. Jerome Robbins Dance Division, The New York Public Library, "Beh: Description," New York Public Library Digital Collections, 2005, http://digitalcollections.nypl.org/items/ffcad140-e7ef-0130-c08a-3c075448cc4b. The next quote is also from this source.

17. René de Nebesky-Wojkowitz, *Tibetan Religious Dances* (New Delhi: Paljor Publications, 1997), 1.

18. Cathy Cantwell, "The Earth Ritual: Subjugation and Transformation of the Environment," *Revue d'Etudes Tibétaines* 7 (April 2005): 4–21.

19. Khenpo Tashi, interview by author, Paro, Bhutan, March 8, 2014.

20. René de Nebesky-Wojkowitz, *Tibetan Religious Dances* (New Delhi: Paljor Publications, 1997), 1–4.

21. Joseph Houseal, "The Dragon's Gift: The Sacred Arts of Bhutan," Core of Culture website, http://www.coreofculture.org/the-dragons-gift.html.

22. Wangchuk, interview by author, at the Punakha Tshechu, Punakha, Bhutan, March 12, 2014..

23. Melvyn C. Goldstein, William Siebenschuh, and Tashi Tsering, *The Struggle for Modern Tibet: The Autobiography of Tashi Tsering* (Armonk, NY: M.E. Sharpe, 1997), 11.

24. Dr. Diana Natalicio, interview by author, UTEP Office of the President, El Paso, TX, August 29, 2014.

25. Samten G. Karmay, "Dorje Lingpa and His Rediscovery of the 'Gold Needle' in Bhutan," *Journal of Bhutan Studies* 2, no. 2 (2000): 4–5.

26. Judith Lynne Hanna, *Dancing to Learn: The Brain's Cognition, Emotion, and Movement* (Lanham, MD: Rowman & Littlefield, 2015), 40.

27. Khenpo Tashi, email message to author, November 26, 2015.

28. See, for example, Cathy Cantwell, "A Tibetan Buddhist Ritual in a Refugee Monastery," *The Tibet Journal* 10, no. 3 (1985): 14–29; and René de Nebesky-Wojkowitz, *Tibetan Religious Dances* (New Delhi: Paljor Publications, 1997), 26.

29. Dasho Sithel Dorji, *The Origin and Description of Bhutanese Mask Dances* (Thimphu, Bhutan: Dasho Sithel Dorji, 2001), 68–69.

30. Khenpo Tashi, email message to author, April 9, 2014.

31. The video referenced was taken at a much smaller festival at Nabji, which is also the purview of Chakar Lam Dorje. As a result, it may differ slightly from the version I describe. It is, however, essentially the same.

32. Michael Aris, *Sources for the History of Bhutan* (Vienna: Arbeitskreis Für Tibetische und Buddhistische Studien Universität Wien, 1986), 139.

33. Khenpo Tashi, email message to author, January 18, 2018.

Bibliography

Ardussi, John. "Formation of the State of Bhutan ('Brug gzhung) in the 17th Century and Its Tibetan Antecedents." In *The Relationship Between Religion and State ("chos srid zung 'brel") in Traditional Tibet*, edited by C. Cüppers, Research Institute, Monograph Series, vol. 4, 10–27. Lumbini, Nepal: Lumbini International, 2005.

———. "Gyalse Tenzin Rabgye (1638–1696), Artist Ruler of 17th Century Bhutan." In *The Dragon's Gift: The Sacred Arts of Bhutan*, edited by Terese Tse Bartholomew and John Johnston, 88–99. Chicago and Honolulu: Serindia and Honolulu Academy of Arts, 2008.

Aris, Michael. *Bhutan: The Early History of a Himalayan Kingdom*. Warminster, UK: Aris & Phillips, 1979.

———. *Sources for the History of Bhutan*. Vienna: Arbeitskreis Für Tibetische und Buddhistische Studien Universität Wien, 1986, 135–149.

Bentor, Yael. *Consecration of Images and Stupas in Indo-Tibetan Tantric Buddhism*. Leiden, The Netherlands: E. J. Brill, 1996.

Beyer, Stephan. *The Cult of Tara: Magic and Ritual in Tibet*. Berkeley: University of California Press, 1978.

Boord, Martin. Introduction to *The Cult of the Deity Vajra Kilaya: According to Texts of the Northern Treasures of Tibet*, 2–18. Tring, UK: Institute of Buddhist Studies, 1993.

Bhutan Dance Database. Produced by Core of Culture. Created: 2005–2007. New York Public Library Digital Collection. Accessed April 5, 2018. https://digitalcollections.nypl.org/collections/bhutan-dance-project-core-of-culture#/?tab=about. (Enter the dance or subject into search field.)

Cantwell, Cathy. "A Black Hat Ritual Dance." *Bulletin of Tibetology* 28, no. 1 (1992): 12–23. http://www.digitalhimalaya.com/collections/journals/bot/index.php?selection=43.

———. "The Dance of the Guru's Eight Aspects." *The Tibet Journal* 20, no. 4 (1995): 47–63.

———. "A Tibetan Buddhist Ritual in a Refugee Monastery." *The Tibet Journal* 10, no. 3 (1985): 14–29.

———. "The Tibetan Earth Ritual: Subjugation and Transformation of the Environment." *Revue d'Etudes Tibétaines* 7 (April 2005): 4–21.

Chakravarti, Balaram. *A Cultural History of Bhutan*. Vol. 1. Chittaranjan, India: Hilltop Publishers, 1979.

Cuevas, Bryan J. "The 'Calf's Nipple' (*Be'u bum*) of Ju Mipam ('Ju Mi pham): A Handbook of Tibetan Ritual Magic." In *Tibetan Ritual*, edited by José Ignacio Cabezón, 165–186. New York: Oxford University Press, 2009.

De Waal, Frans. "Bodies in Sync." *Natural History Magazine* 118, no. 7 (September 2009): 20–25. http://www.naturalhistorymag.com/features/271555/bodies-in-sync.

Dobson, Elaine. "Dancing on the Demon's Back: The

Dramnyen Dance and Song of Bhutan." Research, University of Canterbury, New Zealand, December 1999/January 2000.

———. "Music for the Black-Necked Cranes of Bhutan." In *Asian Futures Asian Traditions*, edited by Edwina Palmer, 419–430. Folkstone, Kent: Global Oriental, 2005.

Dorji, Dasho Sithel. *The Origin and Description of Bhutanese Mask Dances*. Thimphu, Bhutan: Dasho Sithel Dorji, 2001.

Dowman, Keith. *Sky Dancer: The Secret Life and Songs of the Lady Yeshe Tsogyel*. Ithaca, NY: Snow Lion Publications, 1996.

Ellingson, Terry. "Ancient Indian Drum Syllables and Bu Ston's Sham Pa Ta Ritual." *Ethnomusicology*, 24, No. 3 (1980): 431–452.

Gayley, Holly. Introduction to *The Life and Revelations of Pema Lingpa*, by Pema Lingpa, 1–28. Translated by Sarah Harding. Ithaca, NY: Snow Lion Publications, 2003.

"GNH Policy and Project Screening Tools." Center for Bhutan Studies and Gross National Happiness. Accessed September 26, 2012. http://www.grossnationalhappiness.com/gnh-policy-and-project-screening-tools/.

Goldstein, Joseph. *Mindfulness: A Practical Guide to Awakening*. Boulder, CO: Sounds True, 2013 and 2016.

Goldstein, Melvyn C., William Siebenschuh, and Tashi Tsering. *The Struggle for Modern Tibet: The Autobiography of Tashi Tsering*. Armonk, NY: M. E. Sharpe, 1997.

Gyatso, Tenzin. *The World of Tibetan Buddhism: An Overview of Its Philosophy and Practice*. Translated by Geshe Thupten Jinpa. Boston: Wisdom Publications, 1995.

Hanna, Judith Lynne. "Dance and Religion (Overview)." In *The Encyclopedia of Religion*, 2nd ed., edited by Lindsay Jones, 1–15. New York: Macmillan, 2004.

———. *Dancing to Learn: The Brain's Cognition, Emotion, and Movement*. Lanham, MD: Rowman & Littlefield, 2015: 1–23.

———. "Ethnic Dance Research Guide: Relevant Data Categories." *CORD News* 6, no. 1 (1973): 37–44.

———. "The Representation and Reality of Divinity in Dance." *Journal of the American Academy of Religion* 56, no. 2 (1988): 501–526.

———. *To Dance Is Human: A Theory of Nonverbal Communication*. Chicago: The University of Chicago Press, 1979)

Houseal, Joseph. "The Dragon's Gift: The Sacred Arts of Bhutan." Core of Culture. Accessed August 3, 2016. http://www.coreofculture.org/the-dragons-gift.html.

Iacoboni, Marco. "Mental Mirrors." *Natural History Magazine* 117, no. 4 (May 2008): 34–39. http://www.naturalhistorymag.com/features/28883/mental-mirrors.

Jampel Lhakhang Drub Program. Thimphu, Bhutan: Association of Bhutanese Tour Operators, 2015.

Jerome Robbins Dance Division, The New York Public Library. "Beh." New York Public Library Digital Collections, 2005. http://digitalcollections.nypl.org/items/ffcad140-e7ef-0130-c08a-3c075448cc4b.

———. "Boedra." New York Public Library Digital Collections, 2006. https://digitalcollections.nypl.org/items/005ac760-f877-0130-341e-3c075448cc4b.

———. "Dorje Lingpa Ngacham" [Dorling Nga Cham]. New York Public Library Digital Collections, 2005. https://digitalcollections.nypl.org/items/691de390-e377-0130-3d01-3c075448cc4b.

———. "Dorling Gicham" [Dorling Gi Cham]. New York Public Library Digital Collections, 2005. https://digitalcollections.nypl.orgitems/8c146410-e377-0130-4a5c-3c075448cc4b.

———. "Dorling Pacham." New York Public Library Digital Collections, 2005. https://digitalcollections.nypl.org/items/aad8ada0-e377-0130-e574-3c075448cc4b.

———. "Dramitse Nga Cham." New York Public Library Digital Collections, 2005. https://digitalcollections.nypl.org/items/f15ae620-e511-0130-0058-3c075448cc4b.

———. "Geg-toe Mecham." New York Public Library Digital Collections, 2005. https://digitalcollections.nypl.org/items/61268fe0-8292-0130-03a6-3c075448cc4b.

———. "Guru Tshengye." New York Public Library Digital Collections, 2005. https://digitalcollections.nypl.org/items/25396c00-e7f0-0130-f1ae-3c075448cc4b.

———. "Raksha Mangcham." New York Public Library Digital Collections, 2005. https://digitalcollections.nypl.org/items/1eeacad0-e7f0-0130-d210-3c075448cc4b.

———. "Rig Nga Chudru Pachu Gi Cham" [Rigma Chudruk Cham]. New York Public Library Digital Collections, 2005. https://digitalcollections.nypl.org/items/29ac1bb0-e7f0-0130-67da-3c075448cc4b.

———. "Shinjey Yab Yum" [Shinje Yab-Yum]. New York Public Library Digital Collections, 2005. https://digitalcollections.nypl.org/items/39fc1680-8292-0130-8840-3c075448cc4b.

———. "Thongdrol Jyekha" [Zheng Zhi Pem]. New York Public Library Digital Collections, 2005. https://digitalcollections.nypl.org/items/62780cf0-8292-0130-c86e-3c075448cc4b.

———. "Tsechu Zhanag (Nyer Chig) Cham" [Zhanag Cham]. New York Public Library Digital Collections, 2006. https://digitalcollections.nypl.org/items/d3797af0-f876-0130-e6bf-3c075448cc4b.

———. "Zhabdrung Zednam" [Wang Zhey]. New York Public Library Digital Collections, 2005. https://digitalcollections.nypl.org/items/0834a000-e50d-0130-3a3e-3c075448cc4b.

———. "Zhabdrung Zednam" [Zhungdra]. New York Public Library Digital Collections, 2005. https://digitalcollections.nypl.org/items/a1a61f80-e50f-0130-14e0-3c075448cc4b.

Karmay, Samten G. "Dorje Lingpa and His Rediscovery of the 'Gold Needle' in Bhutan." *Journal of Bhutan Studies* 2, no. 2 (2000): 1–35.

———. "The Man and the Ox: A Ritual for Offering the *glud*." In *The Arrow and the Spindle: Studies in History, Myths, Rituals and Beliefs in Tibet*, 339–379. Kathmandu: Mandala Book Point, 1998.

Kinga, Sonam. "The Attributes and Values of Folk and Popular Songs." *Journal of Bhutan Studies* 3, no. 1 (2003): 132–170.

Landaw, Jonathan, and Andy Weber. *Images of Enlightenment: Tibetan Art in Practice*. Ithaca, NY: Snow Lion Publications, 1993 and 2006.

Marsh, Jason. "Do Mirror Neurons Give Us Empathy?" *Greater Good: The Science of a Meaningful Life*, March 29, 2012. Accessed September 23, 2016. https://greatergood.berkeley.edu/article/item/do_mirror_neurons_give_empathy.

Mayer, Robert. "Geographical and Other Borders in the Symbolism of Padmasambhava." Public talk given at the symposium "Moving Borders: Tibet in Interaction with Its Neighbors," Asia Society, New York, May 4–5, 2018. Accessed November 23, 2018. https://www.academia.edu/37685631/Corrected_version_Geographical_and_Other_Borders_in_the_Symbolism_of_Padmasambhava

McDonald, Ross. "Lyonchhen Jigmi Y Thinley." In *Taking Happiness Seriously: Eleven Dialogues on Gross National Happiness*, 1–11. Thimphu, Bhutan: The Centre for Bhutan Studies, 2010.

Nebesky-Wojkowitz, René de. *Tibetan Religious Dances*. New Delhi: Paljor Publications, 1997 and 2001.

Paro Tshechu Programme. Thimphu, Bhutan: Association of Bhutanese Tour Operators.

Phuntsho, Karma. *The History of Bhutan*. Noida, India: Random House India, 2013.

Pommaret, Francoise. "A Cultural Epiphany: Religious Dances of Bhutan and Their Costumes." *Marg* 66, no. 4 (June 2015): 30–39.

———. "Dances in Bhutan: A Traditional Medium of Information." *Journal of Bhutan Studies* 14 (summer 2006): 26–35.

———. "Local Community Rituals in Bhutan." In

Buddhism Beyond the Monastery: Tantric Practices and Their Performers, edited by Sarah H. Jacoby and Antonio Terrone, 4–7. Leiden, The Netherlands: Brill, 2009.

Pommaret, Francoise, and Tashi Tobgay. "Bhutan's Pervasive Phallus: Is Drupka Kunley Really Responsible?" Accessed November 29, 2015. https://www.academia.edu/3197709/Bhutans_pervasive_phallus_Is_Drubka_Kunley_really_responsible.

Ramachandran, V. S. "The Neurons that Shaped Civilization." TEDIndia, November 2009. TED Talk, 7:37. Accessed April 5, 2018. https://www.ted.com/talks/vs_ramachandran_the_neurons_that_shaped_civilization.

Rechung, J. K. "Notes & Topics: The Concept of Dharmaraja." *Bulletin of Tibetology* 28, no. 1 (1992): 34. http://www.digitalhimalaya.com/collections/journals/bot/index.php?selection=43.

Ricard, Matthieu. *Monk Dancers of Tibet*. Translated by Charles Hastings. Boston and London: Shambhala, 2003.

Rinpoche, H. H. Dudjom. *The Nyingma School of Tibetan Buddhism*. Translated by Gyurme Dorje and Matthew Kapstein. Boston: Wisdom Publications, 2002: 789–792.

Royal Academy of Performing Arts. Thimphu, Bhutan: Ministry of Home and Cultural Affairs of the Royal Government of Bhutan, n.d.

Samuel, Geoffrey. *Civilized Shamans: Buddhism in Tibetan Societies*. Washington, DC: Smithsonian Institution Press, 1993.

Schrempf, Mona. "Taming the Earth—Controlling the Cosmos: Transformation of Space in Tibetan Buddhist and Bonpo Ritual Dances." In *Sacred Spaces and Powerful Places in Tibetan Culture*, edited by T. Huber, 198–224. Dharamsala, India: Library of Tibetan Works and Archives, 1999.

———. "Tibetan Ritual Dances and the Transformation of Space." *The Tibet Journal* 19, no. 2 (1994): 95–120.

Skorupski, Tadeusz. "Tibetan Homa Rites According to the *gTer ma* Tradition," *The Tibet Journal* 20, no. 4 (1995): 2–46.

Tashi, Khenpo Phuntshok. *The Fine Art of Living & Manifesting a Peaceful Death: Primordial Wisdom to Enlighten Our Daily Journey*. Independently published, 2017.

———. *Invoking Happiness: Guide to the Sacred Festivals of Bhutan and Gross National Happiness*. Independently published, 2011.

———. "The Positive Impact of Gomchen Tradition on Achieving and Maintaining Gross National Happiness." *Journal of Bhutan Studies* 12, no. 4 (2005): 75–117.

———. *Three Rising Stars: Amazing Life Stories of the Enlightened Masters of Bhutan*. Thimphu, Bhutan: Druk Odiyana Foundation, 2015.

Tobgay, Tshering. "This Country Isn't Just Carbon Neutral—It's Carbon Negative." TED2016, February 2016. TED Talk, 18:55. Accessed April 5, 2018. https://www.ted.com/talks/tshering_tobgay_this_country_isn_t_just_carbon_neutral_it_s_carbon_negative.

"Thousands Celebrate in Changlimithang," *BBS* [Bhutan Broadcasting System], October 15, 2011. Accessed February 13, 2017. http://www.bbs.bt/news/?p=6754.

Thurman, Robert A. F. Introduction to *Essential Tibetan Buddhism*, 1–45. New York: HarperSanFrancisco, 1996.

———, trans. "Background." In *The Tibetan Book of the Dead*, 5–21. New York: Bantam Books, 1994.

Tulku, Mynak R. "The Sacred Dance-Drama of Bhutan." New York: Asia Society's Performing Arts Program, 1979.

Wangchuck, Ashi Dorji Wangmo. *Treasures of the Thunder Dragon: A Portrait of Bhutan*. New Delhi: Penguin Global, 2007.

Index

Illustrations are indicated by page numbers in **bold**.

Buddhism (*continued*)
   Lama-Yidam-Khandro formulation, 153–154
   as national religion, 15–16
   neuroscience and, 137–138
   Opera Bhutan and, 107
Buli Monastery, **124**, 130, 143
Bumthang (region), 121–122, 123, 127–128

calendar system, 12, 26–27, 59
Cambodia, 117
Carpenè, Aaron, 107, 109, 117
Central Monastic Body, 59, 88
Chakar Lam Dorje, **126**, 127–134
   on continuing traditions, 139, 148
   on fertility rite, 166
   on *Jachung Boechung*, 157
   at Jampa Lhakhang Drub, 143, **144**
   on *Tsogcham*, 155
Chakar Lhakhang Temple, **128**, 128–129, 131–134,
   133–134
cham (sacred dances), 199
   author's initial encounter with, 3–4
   author's research into, 4–8
   cosmology and, 41
   development and spread of, 26–27, 35–36, 43, 99,
     102–103
   future of, 102–103
   gender and, 25, 44–45, 51, 97, 103, 163
   humor in, 27, 32, 97
   innovations in, **99–100**, 99–102
   lay performance of, 37, 43–44, 75, 95–99, **96**, 191, **191**,
     195
   mandala structure and, 37–41, **38–40**, 86, 88, 92
   monk performance of, 43, 75, 88, 95
   musical accompaniment and, 27, 38, 41 (*see also* musi-
     cal accompaniment)
   origins of, 74–75
   pre-Buddhist influence on, 91–92, 123, 125

purpose of, 3, 7, 36–38, 69, 88, 95–96, 140, 171, 198
   as sacred art, 122
   tantric, 37–38, 48
   tshechus performances, 27
   as Vajrayana practice, 35–37
   wrathful energy and, 101
chamjug, 88, 149–150, **151**
chamkhang, 156, 184, 199
champon (cham master), 27, 77, 130, 139, 199
cham tax, 95–96, **96**, 99, 131, 139
chang (alcoholic beverage), 62, 199
Changlimithang Stadium, 186, **187**
chanting. *See* singing and chanting
children participating in dance, 162–163
Chimi Lhaden, **96**, 97
Chimi Rinzin, 148, 153, 162, 170–171, **172**, 184
Choden Mengoen (dance), 50
consecration of thongdrel, 135–142, **136**
COP 21 (21st Session of the United Nations Conference
   of Parties on Climate Change), 192
Core of Culture, 6
costumes and props
   atsaras and, 27
   of Black Hat dancer, 65–66, **68**, 88, **89–91**, 91–92
   of *Dorling Gi Cham*, 178
   gho, 26, 44, 114, 143, 149, 200
   of *Guru Dragpo Tordo*, **169**, 169–170
   of *Guru Tshengye Cham*, 77–79
   of Jumpa Lhakhang Drub, 143
   kira (traditional skirt), 51, 114, 143, 200
   of *Nub Zhey*, 195, **196–197**
   of Opera Bhutan, 111, **112**, 114
   of *Pacham* dance, **174–177**, 175
   as part of ritual, 36
   of *Rigma Chudruk Cham*, **85**, 86
   of *Shinje Yab-Yum*, **158**, 159
   of *Tra Geg*, 141
   of *Zheng Zhi Pem*, 188–190, **188–190**